Double Take

Quilts with That Hopscotch Twist

Heather Willms and Elissa Willms

Martingale®
& COMPANY

DEDICATIONS

To all my friends and family who have supported and encouraged me over the years. Thank you for helping make my dreams come true.

~Elissa

Lorne, there are so many things I would not have done without your encouragement. Thanks for sharing the journey with me!

~Heather

Double Take: Quilts with That Hopscotch Twist
© 2010 by Heather Willms and Elissa Willms

That Patchwork Place® is an imprint of Martingale & Company®.

Martingale & Company
20205 144th Ave. NE
Woodinville, WA 98072-8478 USA
www.martingale-pub.com

Printed in China
15 14 13 12 11 10   8 7 6 5 4 3 2 1

Library of Congress Cataloging-in-Publication Data
Library of Congress Control Number: 2009048261

ISBN: 978-1-56477-981-6

Credits

President & CEO: Tom Wierzbicki
Editor in Chief: Mary V. Green
Managing Editor: Tina Cook
Developmental Editor: Karen Costello Soltys
Technical Editor: Robin Strobel
Copy Editor: Marcy Heffernan
Design Director: Stan Green
Production Manager: Regina Girard
Illustrator: Laurel Strand
Cover & Text Designer: Stan Green
Photographer: Brent Kane

Mission Statement

Dedicated to providing quality products and service to inspire creativity.

Contents

Introduction

This book is the result of some of our favorite design ideas. For each project, one of us created the original design. Once completed, the design was then passed off to the other, only to re-emerge in a different colorway, in a different size, and sometimes as a totally new project!

While we often ask each other for an opinion, it certainly doesn't mean that advice is taken. At times we have both worked in each other's color palette, but once the project was complete, a sigh of relief was heard as we returned to our favorite colors and fabrics.

Sometimes as a mother-daughter design team we ask ourselves, "How can two people with similar genetics see things so differently?" Fortunately, the difference in our perspectives is the strength of our design process!

We have had a lot of fun moving colors, changing block sizes, and creating our own unique designs. Perhaps as you work on the projects in this book, you too will be encouraged to see a pattern or a design with fresh perspective and venture into your own unique creation.

~Elissa and Heather Willms

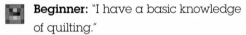

HOPSCOTCH HINT ▶ **HOPSCOTCH PROJECT DIFFICULTY RATING**

Projects are rated according to their level of difficulty.

Beginner: "I have a basic knowledge of quilting."

Intermediate: "I know several quilting techniques, and I no longer sew with a seam ripper in my hand."

Advanced: "I'm a smarty pants when it comes to quilting!"

Page 14

Page 18

Page 22

Page 27

Page 30

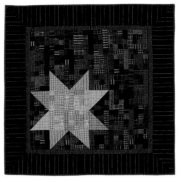

Page 36

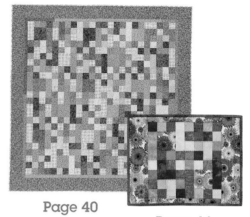

Page 40

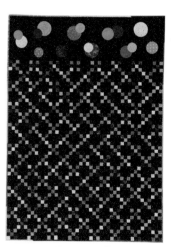

Page 44

Page 46

Page 50

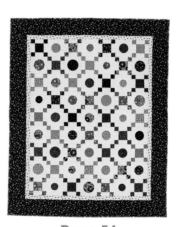

Page 54

Page 58

Page 62

Page 68

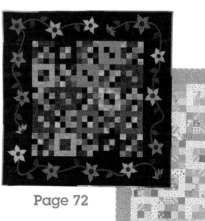

Page 72

Page 77

Let's Get Technical— Quiltmaking Techniques

With a constant flow of new threads and notions on the market, quilters are wise to stay informed regarding what is new to the industry. Imagine missing the introduction of the rotary cutter! Magazines, quilt shops, the Internet, and your local guild are all sources for quilting news and information. That said, we would like to share some of our favorite tips and tricks in the "Hopscotch Hints" boxes as well as basic quiltmaking information to help you succeed in making the projects in this book.

OUR FAVORITE TOOLS

We definitely have some favorite tools that we turn to again and again when quilting and designing.

Rotary cutters: There are many different rotary cutters on the market, so it's important that you find one that works for you. Elissa prefers a standard 45 mm rotary cutter (hers is pink!) and refuses to use the 60 mm pizza-cutter-size rotary cutter that Heather loves.

Pins: It's important to work with pins that are sharp and thin, so they will slide through fabric easily and won't pull on the fabric threads. We love Clover's blue- and yellow-headed patchwork pins for piecing, since we have found them to be sharper than standard quilting pins. The Clover appliqué pins are also sharp and short enough that your thread won't become tangled in them while stitching.

When pin basting quilt tops, make sure you use a pin that is long enough to hold all three layers together.

Needles: We use a range of needles for machine and hand sewing. For machine piecing, Heather prefers microfiber needles, but she uses other needles when thread weights and textures change. When starting a new project, put a new needle into your sewing machine. Every project deserves a sharp needle!

We purchase multisize needle packages for hand sewing so that we're sure to have the right size needle for the job. Beads and buttons require fine needles, while pearl cottons require needles with large eyes. Try a self-threading needle when working with pearl cottons, as you can easily thread the needle without causing the cotton strands to untwist. We like to use straw needles for needle-turn appliqué because the long, narrow shank allows you to easily manipulate the fabric when turning it under freezer paper.

Marking tools: While there are many choices in marking tools, we use thick, wooden soft-chalk pencils, mechanical pencils, and Chaco Liners by Clover. Markings made by the Chaco Liner are easy to remove, and if you're marking a quilting design on a pin-basted top, the marker will roll over the basting pins.

Seam ripper: Heather used to go through a seam ripper a year, but now we use the Clover seam ripper. We call it the "Cadillac" of seam rippers, as it stays sharp through multiple uses. We also like the Fons and Porters seam ripper, which is ergonomically designed and very sharp.

HOPSCOTCH HINT ▸ **THE THREE-RIP RULE**

We have a three-rip rule when it comes to picking out seams. When we're not satisfied with a seam or how something lines up, we'll pick it out and try it again. If it still doesn't meet our standards, we'll pick it out and try again for a total of three tries. After that we leave it, as there are too many quilts waiting to be sewn to devote any more time to a troublesome seam—a very freeing rule for the perfectionist.

Scissors: Sharp scissors are a necessity for quilting. When appliquéing and doing other hand work, having a small pair of scissors that are sharp to the very point is extremely important.

Thread: For piecing, we both prefer 50-weight 100%-cotton thread. Lightweight bobbin threads that aren't 100% cotton are becoming more popular, as are other synthetic fibers for piecing. These finer threads mean that your bobbin can hold more thread, so you can stitch for a longer time before having to change your bobbin!

For machine quilting, we enjoy experimenting with the new soft polyester and rayon threads that don't cut through the cotton fabric, and we love the many yummy thread colors available! We like to use Invisifil thread from Wonderfil when we hand appliqué. This thread is very fine and has a matte finish so you can hardly see the stitches.

CHOOSING FABRICS

There are many projects in this book that use scraps or an assortment of fabrics from your stash. Here are a few principles that can assist you in creating a stunning scrap quilt.

When choosing fabrics for a scrappy-looking project, often the more colors and prints you include, the more you can get away with. If a color or print doesn't coordinate with the three or four fabrics you're working with, it will be noticed. If that same fabric is combined with 20 other fabrics, it will tend to blend a little more. A general rule is that a minimum of 20 different fabrics are needed for an overall scrappy look.

On the other hand, many successful quilts have one fabric that deliberately stands out a little more

than the rest. We call this the zinger. A standout color or print can add life to a dull project. Elissa has no trouble slipping in a zinger or two, but Heather finds it very difficult, because she likes a more blended look.

Scrap quilts are not always as simple and random as they appear. If you look carefully at a scrap quilt, there is often one dominant color or print that ties the quilt together. For example, we have seen stunning Rail Fence quilts where the center strip of every block is a consistent fabric, and the outer strips are assorted scraps.

If you look at "Stash of Stars" on page 68 there are several tan fabrics in the quilt. Using a range within the same basic color family adds texture and zip to a two-color quilt.

WORKING WITH WOOL

There is extensive information on understanding wool in our book, *Christmas Quilts from Hopscotch*, (Martingale & Company, 2008). Here are a few key things to keep in mind:

When wool is felted, the fibers lock together through heat and agitation, so the raw edges of the wool won't unravel. Hand-dyed wools have been through the felting process, and many wools on the market have been felted for you. If the wool you have isn't felted, see "How We Felt Wool" (below) and felt it before appliquéing it to your quilt.

20/80 Woolfelt from National Nonwovens is a less-expensive option due to the small amount of wool content in the felt (20% wool/80% rayon). Generally the greater the wool content, the higher the price. 20/80 Woolfelt is often available in quilt shops and is felted for you. We like to wet 20/80 Woolfelt, and then throw it in the dryer so that it

OPSCOTCH HINT ▶ HOW WE FELT WOOL

1. Set your washer to the hot wash, cool rinse setting. Place the wool in the washing machine, adding a bit of liquid detergent. Make sure the machine agitates a full cycle, because the agitation is what felts the wool.

2. Throw the wool in the drier on a hot setting. Add a towel or two in with the wool to help it dry faster (the towel absorbs some of the moisture). We run fabric with a high wool content through the drier several times to get it completely dry. Take the wool out as soon as it's dry and fold it immediately to avoid wrinkles.

3. If your wool isn't felted as densely as you would like, throw it back in the washing machine and repeat the process.

comes out with a neat bumpy texture. However, don't try to wash 20/80 Woolfelt in your washing machine, as you will be pulling a mess from your washer. If you need to wash your Woolfelt project, gently hand wash it and lay it flat to dry.

When choosing between wool and Woolfelt, there are several things you might want to consider:

- Woolfelt is pre-felted and can be less expensive.

- Availability can be an issue. Can you get the colors you need in wool or Woolfelt? Both come in an array of wonderful colors, but quilt shops can't carry every color available.

- Wool often comes in plaids, houndstooth, and herringbone weaves, while Woolfelt does not.

- Will the project be a seasonal item, or an heirloom to be passed from generation to generation? If you're putting hours and hours of work into a project, you may want to work with wool fabric or felt with a high wool content, which will withstand the test of time.

APPLIQUÉ METHODS

You can choose from a variety of appliqué techniques, but it's important to find a method that works for you. Although you may enjoy a particular technique, on occasion the materials you're using will determine the best method for that project.

Freezer-Paper Needle-Turn Appliqué

1. Trace the patterns on the uncoated side of the freezer paper and cut out on the traced lines. If you are appliquéing a shape more than once, you can reuse your freezer-paper templates several times.

2. Use a hot, dry iron to press the shiny side of the template to the right side of the fabric, leaving approximately ½" between the templates for turning the edges under. Cut out the shapes leaving a scant ¼" margin of fabric around each shape.

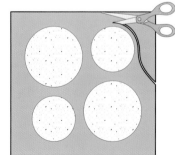

3. Pin the shapes right side up to the right side of the background fabric. Working with approximately 1" of the edge of the shape at a time, turn the edge of the shape under the freezer-paper template using your needle or fingers. Hand stitch in place using a blind hem stitch or slip stitch. If your template becomes loose or comes off during stitching, simply press it in place again. Continue working around the shape until all the edges are turned under and stitched. Knot your thread.

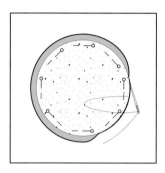

4. Once the shape is appliquéd to the background, remove the template.

When appliquéing larger shapes or shapes that overlap, we like to cut out the background layer of the fabric under the appliquéd shape. This prevents the quilt top from becoming bulky with many layers of fabric. When trimming the background layer of an appliqué shape, pull the background away from the fabric appliquéd on top and make a small slit with your scissors. Then carefully cut the backing away, leaving ¼" of fabric along the stitching line for a seam allowance.

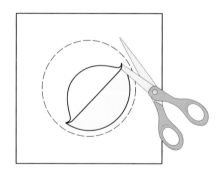

PSCOTCH HINT ## SHOULD I LAYER WOOL APPLIQUÉS?

Because wool can be very thick, it doesn't always work well for layering appliqué shapes. Lay wool appliqué shapes side by side and nudge them right next to each other, rather than overlapping them.

Freezer-Paper Appliqué For Wool

We love using freezer paper for wool appliqué. Wool can be too thick for a fusible product, and freezer paper makes it easy to cut motifs with precision.

1. Follow steps 1 and 2 from Freezer-Paper Needle-Turn Appliqué (page 8), but instead of leaving a scant ¼" margin of wool around each shape, cut out the appliqué shapes along the edge of the freezer paper. Gently remove the freezer paper.

2. Position the appliqué shapes right side up on the right side of the background fabric and pin in place. Stitch around the outside of the shapes using a hand or machine blanket stitch, referring to "Embroidery Stitches" below as needed.

EMBROIDERY STITCHES

We both enjoy handwork and use embroidery to add interesting design elements to our projects. When you choose a thread, remember that the lower the number, the heavier the thread. Pearl cotton is available in both solid and fun variegated colors and comes in several weights (3, 5, 8, and 12). For shapes that are approximately 1" x 1" or larger, we like to use #8 pearl cotton. When using wool, we will go as heavy as #5 pearl cotton because of the bulk of the wool. For intricate appliqué or small appliqué pieces, #12 is our pearl cotton of choice! Variegated three-strand flosses also work well for embroidery.

Don't worry if your embroidery isn't perfect. Handwork adds dimension to a project, and uneven or crooked embroidery adds character! Just be sure that when embroidering over an appliqué motif, you catch both the appliqué piece and the background fabric with each stitch.

Blanket Stitch

While the blanket stitch can be done on many sewing machines, we love the homey look of hand-embroidered blanket stitches around the edges of appliqué motifs.

1. Starting at the edge of the appliqué motif, bring the needle up at A.

2. Insert the needle at B and re-emerge at C, keeping the thread below your work and underneath the needle when it emerges at C. Pull the thread through to form a loop that lies under the emerging thread. The loop should lie snuggly against the fabric without pulling or distorting it.

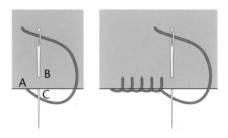

French Knots

French knots make great eyes, buttons, polka dots, and flower centers. (See "Summer Warmth Table Topper" on page 72.)

1. Bring the needle up at A.

2. Hold the needle firmly with your right hand. With your left hand, bring the thread over the needle and wrap the thread around the needle twice, keeping the thread taut. Reinsert the needle at B, right next to A.

3. Hold the wrapped thread right next to the fabric as you pull the thread through to the back of your work. Pull the thread through completely, leaving the knot sitting on the top of the fabric.

FINISHING THE QUILT

Once you have pieced the quilt top, it's time for layering and quilting. In this book, we have included quilts that have been quilted on a regular machine ("A Taste of Turquoise" on page 18), quilted on a long-arm quilting machine ("Peppermint and Chocolate" on page 30) and hand quilted ("Memory Keeper" on page 22). The choice is yours, and fortunately there are many excellent resources for hand quilting and machine quilting. A growing number of amazing long-arm quilters are emerging around the world, and by taking your quilt to a long-arm quilter, you can move on to your next project!

To finish the quilt, you need to make a quilt sandwich, which consists of your quilt top, the batting, and the backing. After securing the layers with pins or by thread basting, hand or machine quilt the layers together. After quilting, the edges will be finished with binding. If you plan to hang your quilt, you might want to add a hanging sleeve.

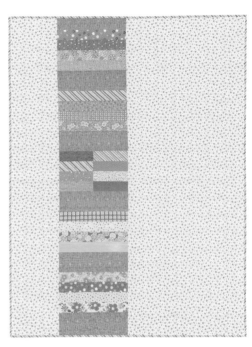

Elissa strip-pieced her leftover Jelly Roll strips and scrap yardage to create a middle panel for the backing of her quilt! How great is that?

HOPSCOTCH HINT ▶ **LOOKING BACK**

- If you would like to hide the quilting on the back of your quilt, choose a print for the backing that is busy and combines several colors. To show off your quilting, choose solids or tone-on-tone prints.

- You will need a backing that is at least 2"–3" larger on all sides than your quilt top to allow for pinning and quilting. If you're using a commercial long-arm quilter to do your quilting, they will thank you for additional yardage around your quilt top.

- Do you have a quilt that is just a little bigger than the width of your backing fabric? Instead of purchasing significantly more fabric to enlarge a quilt back, we like to take the leftover fabric from the front, strip piece it, and add it to the backing. This pieced strip will sometimes enlarge a quilt back enough to fit the top, and it uses up leftover fabrics. We used this technique for the back of "Soaking Up the Sun" on page 77.

- When placing the batting on your quilt backing, make sure there are no loose threads stuck to the batting. Dark threads caught between the batting and the backing could show through light fabrics once the quilt is quilted.

Adding a Hanging Sleeve

We like to sew a hanging sleeve to the upper edge of the quilt before binding it.

1. Cut an 8"-wide strip of fabric equal to the width of your quilt, piecing if necessary. On each short end of the strip, fold ½" to the wrong side, and then fold ½" again to make a hem. Press, and machine stitch. The sleeve should measure about 2" narrower than the width of your quilt.

2. Fold the strip in half lengthwise, wrong sides together. Center and baste the raw edges to the upper edge of the back of your quilt. These raw edges will be secured in the binding.

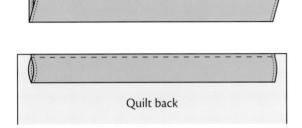

Quilt back

3. Pin the bottom of the sleeve to the quilt back, rolling the edge up ¼". This adds a little extra room for the hanging rod. Slip-stitch the ends and bottom edge of the sleeve to the backing fabric.

Straight-Grain Binding

To prepare your quilt for binding, use a walking foot on your machine to baste a scant ¼" from the edges of the quilt top. This will hold the layers in place and help prevent puckers. Trim the batting and backing to extend ⅛" beyond the quilt top. (See "Creating a Full Binding" hint box below.)

The projects in this book include yardage for double-fold straight-grain binding that is cut 2½" wide.

1. Cut binding strips as instructed for the project you're making. To join the strips, overlap the ends with right sides together as shown. Sew diagonally from corner to corner. Trim the outside corner, leaving a ¼"-wide seam allowance, and press seam allowances to one side.

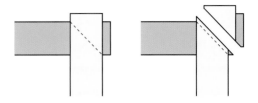

2. When the strips have been sewn together and pressed, cut one end at a 45° angle. Press the binding in half lengthwise, wrong sides together, aligning the raw edges.

3. Beginning with the angled end of the strip, place the binding along one side of the quilt (not at a corner) and align the raw edges of the strip with the raw edge of the quilt top. Leaving the first 8" unstitched, stitch the binding to the quilt using a ¼" seam allowance and the edge of the quilt top as a guide. (The backing and batting will extend ⅛" beyond the edge of the quilt top and the binding.) At the first corner, stop sewing ¼" from the quilt edge and backstitch. Clip the thread and remove the quilt from the machine.

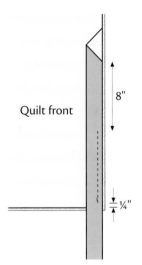

Quilt front

8"

¼"

4. Rotate the quilt 90°, so that you're ready to sew down the next side. To miter the corners, fold

---

CREATING A FULL BINDING

After quilting, use a rotary cutter and ruler to trim the backing and batting. Lay the ruler along the edge of the quilt top and cut so that ⅛" of batting and backing extends beyond the raw edge of the quilt top. When you attach the binding, align the edge of the strip with the edge of the quilt top. The extra width of batting creates a full binding. Otherwise, the binding might feel thin and limp. When sewing the binding, be sure to sew ¼" from the raw edge of the quilt top, not the edge of the batting.

the binding strip up so the edge of the binding is even with the edge of the quilt. Then fold the binding down, keeping the fold even with the top edge of the quilt. Begin with a backstitch at the fold of the binding and continue stitching along the edge of the quilt top, mitering each corner as you come to it.

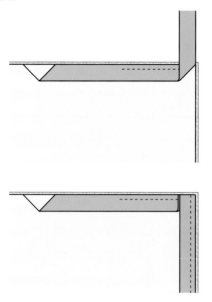

5. Stop sewing about 10" from where you began stitching. Clip the thread and remove your quilt from the machine. Lay the beginning tail flat on the quilt top. Overlap the end of the binding over the beginning. Trim the end of the binding at a 45° angle so the overlap measures ½". Sew the two ends together, as shown, and trim if needed, leaving a ¼" seam allowance. Press the seam allowances to one side; then refold the binding in half and press the fold. Lay the binding flat along the quilt edge and stitch in place.

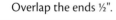

Overlap the ends ½".

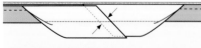

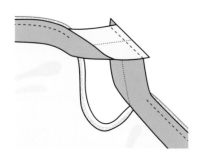

6. Fold the edge of the binding to the back of the quilt and pin in place so that the folded edge covers the row of machine stitching. Using thread that matches your binding, hand stitch the binding to the quilt back, mitering each corner. If you plan to add a label, attach it before hand sewing the binding in place.

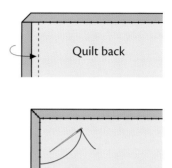

Quilt back

Bias Binding

Bias binding allows you to make use of directional fabrics like stripes and plaids, as we've done on many of the projects in this book.

1. To make bias strips for binding, open up your binding fabric and lay it in a single layer on the cutting mat. Align the 45° line on your rotary-cutting ruler with one of the selvage edges of the fabric.

2. Cut along the ruler edge to trim off the corner. Cut 2½"-wide strips, measuring from the edge of the first cut.

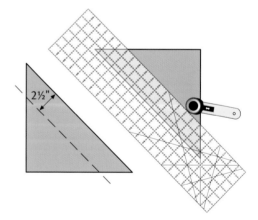

2½"

DIAGONAL PIECING OF BORDERS AND BINDINGS

We always join our border and binding strips at a 45° angle when sewing the strips end to end. A seam with a 45° angle encourages the viewer's eye to keep moving. If the seam runs at a right angle to the quilt, it tends to stop the eye, and the viewer will become more aware of the seam.

3. Sew the strips end to end to make one long binding strip. Note that most of the strips will already have a 45° angle at the end, so you won't need to trim off the outside corners when sewing the strips together.

4. Apply the binding as for "Straight-Grain Binding" on page 11.

Labels

Once a quilt is finished, it's important to take the time to create a label. Not only does a label identify a quilt if it becomes lost, but it also documents the history of the quilt and increases meaning for the recipient of a quilted gift.

Basic information on a label should include:

- The name of the quilt
- The date it was completed (thankfully not when it was started)
- The name of the quilter
- The place the quilt was made

We also like to add any interesting information about the quilt; for example, if it was made for a special occasion or a special person.

Some fabric manufacturers make printed fabric labels. You can also use muslin or even a light-colored fabric from your quilt top for your labels. We've pieced labels with strips of fabric from the quilt top, and we've also used leftover blocks. Once you've created a label, turn the top and right edges of the label under ¼" and press. Write on your label using a Pigma pen. These permanent pens can be found at any scrapbook or stationery store. A Pigma pen is waterproof and will not bleed into the fabric.

We find it easiest to attach the label after the binding has been machine stitched to the quilt top, but before it's been hand sewn to the quilt back.

1. Place the label at the lower-left corner of the quilt back and pin in place. Machine baste a scant ¼" from the edge of the quilt, sewing along the bottom and left edges of the label. Stop sewing at least ¼" from the corner of the quilt. The basting stitches should run right alongside the stitching line (in the seam allowance) for the binding.

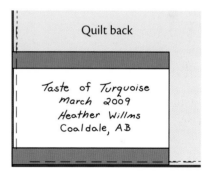

2. Hand stitch the label to the quilt back along the upper and right sides of the label. Then fold the binding over the raw edges of the quilt and label and hand sew the binding to the back of the quilt.

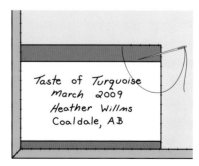

Pinwheel Pizzazz

Dig into your stash to create this colorful quilt of pinwheels with a funky black-and-white twist. While Elissa is not a fan of square quilts, she intentionally made this quilt the size of a standard shower curtain. Check out "Shower Curtain with Pizzazz" on page 17 to find out how to brighten your bathroom with a quilted shower curtain.

Finished quilt: 71" x 71"
Finished block: 10" x 10"
Skill level:

MATERIALS

*Yardage is based on 42"-wide fabrics,
unless otherwise specified.*

1 yard *each* of assorted blue, yellow, orange, pink,
   purple, and green prints for Pinwheel blocks
1 yard *total* of assorted black-with-white prints for
   block corners
1 yard *total* of assorted white-with-black prints for
   block corners
¾ yard of black-and-white print for borders
⅔ yard of black-and-multicolored print for binding
4¾ yards of fabric for backing
77" x 77" piece of batting

CUTTING

All measurements include ¼" seam allowances.

From *each set* of assorted blue, yellow, orange, pink,
purple, and green print, cut:
28 squares, 5⅞" x 5⅞" (168 total)

From the assorted black-with-white prints,
cut a *total* of:
84 squares, 3½" x 3½"

From the assorted white-with-black prints,
cut a *total* of:
84 squares, 3½" x 3½"

From the black-and-white border print, cut:
4 strips, 5½" x 42"

From the black-and-multicolored print, cut:
8 strips, 2½" x 42"

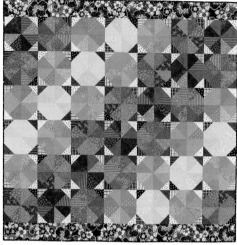

Pieced and quilted by Elissa

CREATING THE BLOCKS

1. Using a mechanical pencil or your favorite
marking tool, draw a line diagonally from one corner
to the opposite corner on the backs of 14 of the blue
5⅞" squares.

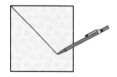

2. Lay a marked blue square on top of an unmarked
blue square, right sides together. Sew ¼" on either side
of the drawn line, cut on the line, and press open
to make two half-square-triangle units, 5½" x 5½".
Repeat with the remaining blue squares to create a
total of 28 blue half-square-triangle units.

3. Sew four half-square-triangle units together following the diagram below to create seven blue pinwheels.

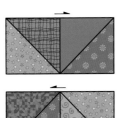

Make 7 blue pinwheels.

4. Repeat steps 1–3 with the remaining 5⅞" squares to create seven pinwheels in each color (42 total).

5. Mark the back of all the black-with-white squares, as in step 1. With right sides together, lay a black-with-white square on a corner of a blue pinwheel, aligning two sides of the black square with the outside edges of the pinwheel. Sew on the marked line.

Repeat on the remaining three corners of the pinwheel. Trim the seam allowances to ¼" and press the black-with-white triangles toward the corners of the block.

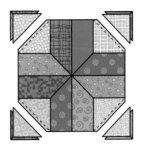

6. Using the remaining black-with-white squares, repeat step 5 for all of the blue, pink, and yellow pinwheels.

Make 7 blue. Make 7 pink.

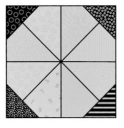

Make 7 yellow.

7. Mark the 3½" white-with-black squares as you did the black-with-white squares. Add white-with-black squares to the corners of all of the green, orange and purple pinwheels as in step 5. Trim the seam allowances to ¼" and press them toward the center of the blocks.

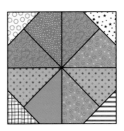

Make 7 green. Make 7 orange.

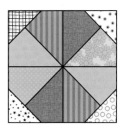

Make 7 purple.

ASSEMBLING THE QUILT TOP

1. Arrange the blocks according to the diagram at right. Sew the blocks in rows, pressing the seam allowances toward the blocks with the black corner triangles.

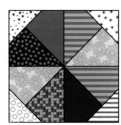

2. Sew the rows together to create the center of the quilt. Press.

3. Sew the 5½"-wide black-and-white strips end to end to create one long strip. Measure the width of your quilt top through the center, not along the edges. Cut two strips to fit. Sew to the top and bottom of the quilt. Press seam allowances toward the strips.

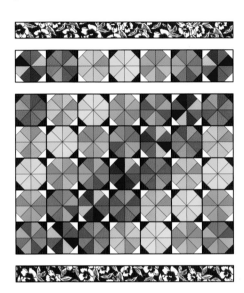

FINISHING THE QUILT

1. If necessary, mark your quilt for quilting. Layer the top with batting and backing; baste.

2. Hand or machine quilt as desired. Elissa chose to use a swirly quilting pattern in the borders and a floral design in the blocks.

3. Add a hanging sleeve if you plan to hang your quilt.

4. Using the 2½"-wide black-and-multicolored binding strips and referring to "Straight-Grain Binding" on page 11 as needed, bind your quilt.

5. Label your quilt.

SHOWER CURTAIN WITH PIZZAZZ

Add a personal touch and some spark to your bathroom by turning your Pinwheel Pizzazz quilt top into a shower curtain. While a quilt is too heavy to hang on shower hooks, quilting your top without batting will make it light enough to use as a shower curtain.

Or, skip the quilting completely and create a shower curtain by making what looks like a very big pillowcase out of your quilt top. Reinforce the top of the curtain by fusing a strip of 2" heavyweight interfacing to the wrong side of the top edge of your quilt. With right sides together, sew the backing fabric to the quilt top by stitching up one side, across the top and back down the other side. Turn right sides out, and press. Leave the bottom of the shower curtain open, but hem the bottom edge. Topstitch ¼" from the edge along the three sewn sides of the curtain.

If you require a 72" shower curtain length, measure the length of your quilt before the borders are added. Cut the borders wide enough to give you the length you require. Remember to add 1¼" for the seam allowance (½" will be lost when you sew the edge of your borders to the top and bottom of the quilt and ¼" will be lost when you sew the top of the quilt to the quilt back). Add an additional ½" for the hem at the bottom of the shower curtain (¼" turned under twice).

Before sewing buttonholes or adding grommets for the shower hooks, mark where you want the holes and make sure they're spaced evenly across the top of the quilt. Typically, there are 12 holes spaced about 6" apart, with the first and last holes placed 1½" from the edges.

Reinforce the top of the curtain by sewing 1½" from the top edge. Be sure to use a plastic shower-curtain liner to keep your personalized shower curtain dry.

A Taste of Turquoise

Heather turned the Pinwheel Pizzazz blocks into a new design by using only three colors and changing the color placement of some of the corner triangles. This runner makes a great gift or a treat for your own home.

Finished quilt: 25½" x 49½"
Finished blocks: 6" x 6"
Skill level: ▦▦

MATERIALS

Yardage is based on 42"-wide fabric.

1 yard *total* of assorted turquoise prints for blocks
½ yard *total* of assorted brown prints for blocks
⅜ yard of cream print for block corners and narrow
  border
⅞ yard of brown print for border and binding
1¾ yards of turquoise fabric for backing
31" x 55" piece of batting

CUTTING

All measurements include ¼" seam allowances.

From the assorted turquoise prints, cut a *total* of:
72 squares, 3⅞" x 3⅞"

From the assorted brown prints, cut a *total* of:
12 squares, 3⅞" x 3⅞"
24 squares, 2" x 2"

From the cream print, cut:
3 strips, 2" x 42", cut into 48 squares, 2" x 2"
4 strips, 1" x 42"

From the brown print for border and binding, cut:
4 strips, 3½" x 42"
4 strips, 2½" x 42"

Pieced and quilted by Heather

CREATING THE BLOCKS

1. Follow steps 1–3 of "Creating the Blocks" on page 15 for Pinwheel Pizzazz to make 18 turquoise pinwheels and 3 brown pinwheels.

2. Following the placement guide below and step 5 on page 16 from Pinwheel Pizzazz, add the 2" cream and 2" brown squares to the turquoise pinwheels. Make eight blocks with four cream corners, two blocks with four brown corners and eight blocks with two cream corners and two brown corners (see diagrams below). The three brown Pinwheel blocks will not have 2" squares sewn to them, but will remain as plain Pinwheel blocks.

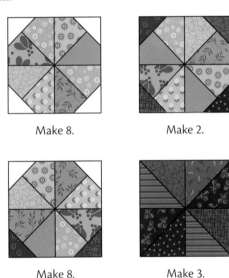

Make 8.   Make 2.

Make 8.   Make 3.

ASSEMBLING THE QUILT TOP

1. Sew the blocks together following the diagram at right. Sew the blocks into rows, pressing the seam allowances in alternate directions from row to row.

2. Sew the 1"-wide cream strips end to end to create one long strip. Measure the length of the runner through the center. Cut two cream strips to fit. Sew them to each side of the runner. Press seam allowances toward the cream print.

3. Measure the width of the runner through the center (including the cream borders you added in step 2). Cut two cream strips to fit. Sew to the top and bottom of the runner. Press seam allowances toward the cream fabric.

4. Repeat steps 2 and 3 with the 3½"-wide brown strips.

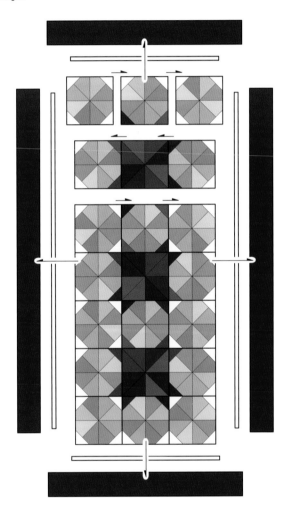

FINISHING THE QUILT

1. If necessary, mark your quilt for quilting. Layer the top with batting and backing; baste.

2. Hand or machine quilt as desired. Heather chose to stitch in the ditch for the center of the runner, and quilt lines 1" apart in the borders.

3. Add a hanging sleeve if you plan to hang this runner as a wall quilt.

4. Using the 2½"-wide brown print strips and referring to "Straight-Grain Binding" on page 11 as needed, bind your runner.

5. Label your runner.

HOPSCOTCH HINT

A TASTE OF TURQUOISE IN A HURRY

While it's never fun to have to eat on the run, as quilters there are times when we want to make a gift but have to create it in a hurry. If you want to make Taste of Turquoise but aren't sure you have time for all the piecing, leave each pinwheel as a solid square of fabric!

Start with 18 squares, 6½" x 6½", of assorted prints in one color and three squares, 6½" x 6½", of assorted prints in a second color. Beginning with step 2 of "Creating the Blocks" on page 15, assemble the runner as directed. While this runner will not be quite as textured as the one with pieced pinwheels, you will still achieve fabulous results on a tight time schedule.

Memory Keeper

Although this looks like a scrappy little wall quilt, it's actually the keeper of many memories. The fabrics used in this quilt come from Heather's scrap bag and remind her of quilting friends and a variety of quilting experiences. The quilt contains fabrics from block exchanges, from a quilting friend who has passed away, from projects for friends, and even an original piece of fabric from when she and Elissa opened Hopscotch Quilt Shop. If your scrap bag does not contain a wealth of memories, trade fabrics with a few friends, your sewing group, or your guild to make your own Memory Keeper quilt.

Finished quilt: 24¼" x 29"

Block size: 4" x 4"

Skill level: ▦ ▦

MATERIALS

Yardage is based on 42"-wide fabric.

½ yard *total* of assorted light prints

⅜ yard *total* of assorted dark prints

⅓ yard of black print for sashing

⅛ yard of red checked fabric for corner posts

⅓ yard of green print of outer border

½ yard of red plaid for binding

1 yard of fabric for backing

30" x 35" of batting

CUTTING

All measurements include ¼" seam allowances.

Each individual block uses the same light print for all the light pieces within that block. Each Turnstile, Ohio Star, and Spinning Star block uses the same dark print for all the dark pieces within that block (except for one renegade Turnstile block with 4 different dark prints). Each Hourglass block has two dark prints for the dark pieces.

The cutting instructions are for one block only. Cut five of each block, using different fabrics for each block.

Turnstile Block

From *one* of the light prints, cut:

1 square, 3¼" x 3¼"; cut into quarters diagonally to yield 4 triangles

2 squares, 2⅞" x 2⅞"; cut each square in half diagonally to yield 4 triangles

From *one* of the dark prints, cut:

1 square, 3¼" x 3¼"; cut into quarters diagonally to yield 4 triangles

Ohio Star Block

From *one* of the light prints, cut:

1 square, 3¼" x 3¼"; cut into quarters diagonally to yield 4 triangles

4 squares, 1½" x 1½"

From *one* of the dark prints, cut:

1 square, 2½" x 2½"

4 squares, 1⅞" x 1⅞"; cut each square in half diagonally to yield 8 triangles

Spinning Star Block

From *one* of the light prints, cut:

2 squares, 1⅞" x 1⅞"

4 squares, 1½" x 1½"

2 rectangles, 1½" x 2½"

From *one* of the dark prints, cut:

2 squares, 1⅞" x 1⅞"

1 square, 2½" x 2½"

Hourglass Block

From *one* of the light prints, cut:

2 squares, 2⅞" x 2⅞"; cut each square in half diagonally to yield 4 triangles

From *one* of the dark prints, cut:

1 square, 2⅞" x 2⅞"; cut in half diagonally to yield 2 triangles

From a *different* dark print, cut:

1 square, 2⅞" x 2⅞"; cut in half diagonally to yield 2 triangles

Sashing, Borders, and Binding

From the black print, cut:

7 strips, 1¼" x 42"; crosscut into 49 rectangles, 1¼" x 4½"

From the red checked fabric, cut:

1 strip, 1¼" x 42"; crosscut into 30 squares, 1¼" x 1¼"

From the green print, cut:

3 strips, 2½" x 42"

From the red plaid, cut:

2½"-wide bias strips, enough to yield 112"

Pieced and hand quilted by Heather

TWO-COLOR QUILTS

If you have a collection of two different colored prints (for example, creams and blues), this is the perfect quilt to dabble, as it can be made with light fabrics for the background and dark fabrics for the design. These design fabrics can be either medium or dark in value as long as they contrast with the light background fabrics.

CREATING THE BLOCKS

Piecing instructions are for one block. Make five each of the four different blocks.

Turnstile Block

1. Sew a small light triangle to a small dark triangle along a short side. It's important that you piece your triangle with the light print on top each time; otherwise, the light and dark triangles will not consistently be on the same side. Press the seam allowances toward the dark triangle. Repeat to create a total of 4 triangle units.

Sew with light
triangle on top.

Make 4
for each block.

2. Sew the block pieces together following the illustration below. Make four more Turnstile blocks using different light and dark prints in each, so that none of the blocks are the same.

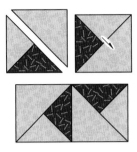
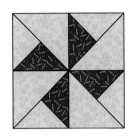

Make 5.

If you would like to vary the dark prints in one of your Turnstile blocks, from one print, cut one $2\frac{7}{8}$" square, and then cut it in half diagonally. Repeat with a second print. This will give you a two-color Turnstile block. You could also cut two $3\frac{1}{4}$" squares from four different prints, and then cut each square twice diagonally to yield four triangles from each square. Mix them to make four 4-color Turnstile blocks. One of the Turnstile blocks in our quilt is made of four different-colored prints.

Ohio Star Block

1. Sew a small dark triangle on either side of a light triangle as shown to create a flying-geese unit. Press seam allowances toward the dark triangles. Repeat to make a total of four flying-geese units.

Flying-geese unit.
Make 4
for each block.

2. Sew the block pieces together following the illustration below. Make four more Ohio Star blocks using different light and dark prints in each, so none of the blocks are the same.

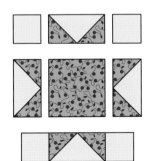
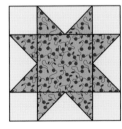

Make 5.

For a scrappier look, consider making the center of your Ohio Star block one fabric and the star points from one or more different fabrics.

Spinning Star Block

1. Using a mechanical pencil or your favorite marking tool, draw a diagonal line from corner to corner on the back of each light 1⅞" square. Lay a marked square on top of a dark 1⅞" square, right sides together, and sew ¼" on either side of the marked line.

2. Cut on the marked line and open the units. Press the seam allowances toward the dark print. Repeat with remaining dark and light 1⅞" squares to make a total of four half-square-triangle units.

Half-square-triangle unit.
Make 4
for each block.

3. Sew the block pieces together following the illustration below. To add variety, Heather reversed the placement of the triangles in the purple block, causing the star to spin in the opposite direction. Make four more Spinning Star blocks using different light and dark prints in each, so none of the blocks are the same.

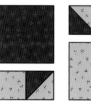
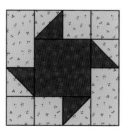

Make 5.

Hourglass Block

1. Lay a dark triangle on top of a light triangle, right sides together. Sew along the long side of the triangles. Press seam allowances toward the dark triangle. Repeat with remaining dark and

light triangles, pressing seam allowances toward the dark triangles to make a total of four half-square-triangle units.

Half-square-triangle units.
Make 2 of each color
for one block.

2. Sew the half-square-triangle units together following the illustration below. Make four more Hourglass blocks using different light and dark prints in each, so none of the blocks are the same.

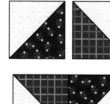
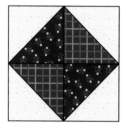

Make 5.

ASSEMBLING THE QUILT TOP

1. Sew the pieced blocks and black sashing rectangles together in rows as shown, pressing all the seam allowances toward the sashing. Sew black sashing rectangles and red squares together in rows, pressing all seam allowances toward the sashing. Sew the rows together and press.

2. Sew the green print strips together end to end to make a continuous strip. From the long strip, cut two 2½" x 25" strips and sew one to each side of the quilt. Press seam allowances toward the border strips. Cut two 2½" x 24¼" strips and sew one each to the top and bottom of the quilt. Press seam allowances toward the border strips.

FINISHING THE QUILT

1. If necessary, mark your quilt for quilting. Layer the top with batting and backing; baste

2. Hand or machine quilt as desired. Heather chose to hand quilt her quilt, stitching ¼" away from the pieced edges of the blocks. She quilted two parallel lines in the borders.

3. Add a hanging sleeve if you plan to hang your quilt.

4. Using the red plaid 2½"-wide bias strips and referring to "Bias Binding" on page 12 as needed, bind your quilt.

5. Label your quilt. If it's a quilt that uses memorable pieces of fabric from friends and family, be sure to note them on your quilt label.

HOPSCOTCH HINT ▶ ## TO HAND QUILT OR NOT TO HAND QUILT

Although Heather thinks hand quilting is the best quilting, time is a huge factor when considering whether to hand quilt a project. We take several things into consideration when making this decision:

- Is the quilt for a special occasion or event (such as a wedding)? Since Memory Keeper is a quilt that represents friends, family, and special memories, Heather decided to hand quilt the quilt.

- Is the quilt going to a home where it will be cherished and well kept for years to come? If you're making a quilt that will be going to a dorm room to have soda and popcorn spilled on it, machine quilting is a much more sensible option.

- Will the quilt be washed repeatedly, especially in a washing machine? A baby quilt that is going to be used will need repeated washings. Hand quilting may not stand up to its every day wear and tear.

- Is there a lot of handwork on the quilt? When a quilt has a lot of hand appliqué and many hours have been invested, we always feel it deserves to be hand quilted.

Scatterbrained Eye Spy

Elissa started this quilt early in her quilting years, "borrowing" fabric from Heather's stash. Using simple plain and pieced blocks, this quilt is quick and easy to make. "Eye Spy" quilts use a variety of novelty prints and are designed for children. Children can spend hours looking for bugs, cars, food, etc. If you don't have many prints that are suitable for an Eye Spy quilt, trade with friends and fellow guild members to increase your variety—and theirs!

Finished quilt: 54½" x 66½"
Finished block: 6" x 6"
Skill level:

Pieced and quilted by Elissa

MATERIALS

Yardage is based on 42"-wide fabric.

3¼ yards *total* of assorted novelty prints for plain blocks

⅜ yard of white fabric for pieced blocks

⅜ yard *total* of assorted dark prints for pieced blocks

⅝ yard of multicolored print for binding

3¾ yards of flannel for backing

60" x 72" of batting

CUTTING

All measurements include ¼" seam allowances.
Cutting instructions are for one block only.

Turnstile Block
(Cut 1 block.)

From the white fabric, cut:

1 square, 4¼" x 4¼"; cut into quarters diagonally to yield 4 triangles

2 squares 3⅞" x 3⅞"; cut each square in half diagonally to yield 4 triangles total

From *one* dark print, cut:

1 square, 4¼" x 4¼"; cut into quarters diagonally to yield 4 triangles

Ohio Star Block
(Cut 2 blocks.)

From the white fabric, cut:

1 square, 4¼" x 4¼"; cut into quarters diagonally to yield 4 triangles

4 squares, 2" x 2"

From *one* dark print, cut:

4 squares, 2⅜" x 2⅜"; cut each square in half diagonally to yield 8 triangles total

1 square, 3½" x 3½"

Spinning Star Block
(Cut 2 blocks.)

From the white fabric, cut:

2 squares, 2⅜" x 2⅜"

4 squares, 2" x 2"

2 rectangles, 2" x 3½"

From *one* dark print, cut:

2 squares, 2⅜" x 2⅜"

1 square, 3½" x 3½"

Hourglass Block
(Cut 2 blocks.)

From the white fabric, cut:

2 squares, 3⅞" x 3⅞"; cut each square in half diagonally to yield 4 triangles total

From *one* dark print, cut:

1 square, 3⅞" x 3⅞"; cut in half diagonally to yield 2 triangles

From a different dark print, cut:

1 square, 3⅞" x 3⅞"; cut in half diagonally to yield 2 triangles

Unpieced Blocks and Binding

From the assorted novelty prints for plain blocks, cut:

92 squares, 6½" x 6½"

From the multicolored print, cut:

7 strips, 2½" x 42"

CREATING THE BLOCKS

For the pieced blocks, Elissa made two of each block used in "Memory Keeper" on pages 22–26, except for the Turnstile block. She made only one Turnstile block for a total of seven pieced blocks. Follow the cutting instructions on page 23 for the pieced 6½" x 6½" blocks in this quilt, and then follow the piecing instructions in Memory Keeper to sew the blocks together. Create your own unique quilt by adding or deleting different pieced blocks.

Instructions for assembling the different blocks begin on the following pages:

- Turnstile—page 24
- Ohio Star—page 24
- Spinning Star—page 24
- Hourglass—page 25

Elissa deviated from the Hourglass blocks in Memory Keeper by rotating two of the half-square-triangle units. If you want your Hourglass blocks to look like Elissa's, make the four half-square-triangle units according to the directions in Memory Keeper, but sew them together referring to the illustration below.

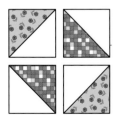 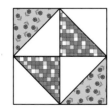

ASSEMBLING THE QUILT TOP

Sew the blocks and assorted novelty squares together following the diagram below. Sew the blocks in rows, pressing seam allowances in alternate directions from row to row. Sew the rows together.

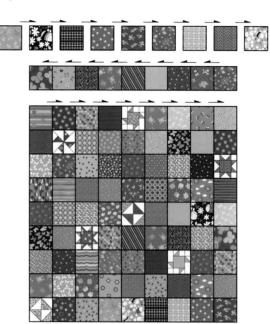

FINISHING THE QUILT

1. If necessary, mark your quilt for quilting. Layer the top with batting and backing; baste

2. Hand or machine quilt as desired. Elissa quilted a continuous design of loops, dragonflies, and butterflies using her long-arm quilting machine.

3. Add a hanging sleeve if you plan to hang your quilt.

4. Using the 2½"-wide multicolored print strips and referring to "Straight-Grain Binding" on page 11 as needed, bind your quilt.

5. Label your quilt. If your quilt has been made for a special little someone, be sure to include their name on the label.

Peppermint and Chocolate

Heather and Elissa both love the offset star in this quilt. It originally started in the middle of the quilt but made its way to the corner with stunning results! This amazing quilt is charm square and Jelly Roll friendly.

Finished quilt: 80½" x 88½"
Finished block: 8" x 8"
Skill level:

MATERIALS

Yardage is based on 42"-wide fabric.

2 yards of brown-with-green print for borders

1⅞ yards in *each of the four colors* of assorted pink, purple, green, and blue prints for blocks, borders, and binding

⅝ yard of brown-with-pink print for star points

½ yard *total* of assorted brown prints for blocks

7⅞ yards of fabric for backing

86" x 94" of batting

CUTTING

All measurements include ¼" seam allowances.

From the assorted pink, purple, green, and blue prints, cut a *total* of:

47 strips, 2½" x 42"

9 strips, 4½" x 42"; cut into 72 squares, 4½" x 4½"

From *each* of 3 pink, 3 purple, 3 green, and 3 blue prints, cut:

2 strips, 2½" x 42" (24 total); cut *each strip* into:

 3 rectangles, 2½" x 8½" (72 total)

 3 rectangles, 2½" x 4½" (72 total)

From the assorted brown prints, cut a *total* of:

32 squares, 2½" x 2½"

2 squares, 4½" x 4½"

From *each* of two of the assorted brown prints, cut:

2 rectangles, 2½" x 4½" (4 total)

2 rectangles, 2½" x 8½" (4 total)

From the brown-with-pink print, cut:

8 squares, 8½" x 8½"

From the brown-with-green print, cut:

16 strips, 2½" x 42"

5 strips, 4½" x 42"; cut into 38 squares, 4½" x 4½"

Pieced by Elissa and quilted by Karen Young

CREATING BLOCK A

1. Using 18 of the assorted 2½" x 42" strips, sew two strips of different colors together along their length to make one strip set. Repeat, using different color combinations, to make a total of nine assorted strip sets. Press seam allowances toward the darker fabrics.

2. Cut the strip sets into 2½"-wide units. Each strip set yields 16 units, for a total of 144 two-square units.

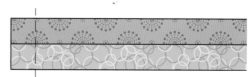

2½"

Make 9 strip sets.
Cut 144 units.

3. Sew four different-colored 2½" x 42" strips together along the length of the strips. Repeat, using different color combinations, to make a total of five assorted strip sets. Press seam allowances in one direction. Cut the strip sets into 2½"-wide units. Each strip set yields 16 units for a total of 80 four-square units.

2½"

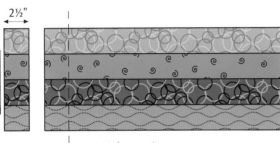

Make 5 strip sets.
Cut 80 units.

4. Sew a two-square unit from step 2 to each side of a pink, purple, green, or blue 4½" square. Press seam allowances toward the center square. Set the unused two-square units aside for making block B.

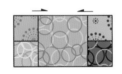

5. Sew a four-square unit from step 3 to the top and bottom of the block. Press seam allowances toward the center square.

6. Repeat steps 4 and 5 to create 34 of block A.

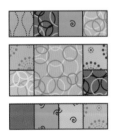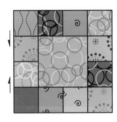

Block A.
Make 34.

CREATING BLOCK B

1. Sew together two of the remaining two-square units to create a four-patch unit as shown. Repeat to make 34 four-patch units. You will have eight unused two-square units.

Make 34.

2. Select two 2½" x 4½" rectangles and two 2½" x 8½" rectangles from the same fabric. Sew the 2½" x 4½" rectangles to the top and bottom of a four-patch unit. Press the seam allowances toward the rectangles.

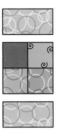

3. Sew the 2½" x 8½" rectangles to each side of the four-patch unit. Press the seam allowances toward the rectangles.

4. Repeat steps 2 and 3 to make 34 of block B. You will have eight unused rectangles.

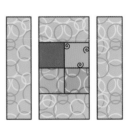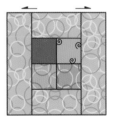

Block B.
Make 34.

CREATING THE STAR

1. Arrange one brown 4½" square and 12 brown 2½" squares to make block A as shown below. Sew the side 2½" squares together, and then sew them to either side of the center square. Press seam allowances as shown. Sew the four squares for the top and four squares for the bottom into rows, and press as shown. Sew the rows to the top and bottom of the quilt block. Repeat to make a total of 2 brown block A.

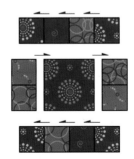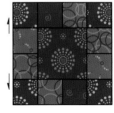

Brown block A.
Make 2.

2. Arrange four brown 2½" squares, two brown 2½" x 4½" rectangles, and two brown 2½" x 8½" rectangles to make block B as shown. Sew the 2½" squares together to make a four-patch unit. Sew the 2½" x 4½" rectangles to the top and bottom of the four-patch unit and press seam allowances toward the rectangles. Sew the 2½" x 8½" rectangles to the sides of the block, again pressing seam allowances toward the rectangles. Repeat to make a total of two brown block B.

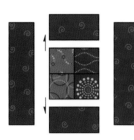

Brown block B.
Make 2.

3. Using a mechanical pencil or your favorite making tool, draw a diagonal line from corner to corner on the back of each brown 8½" square.

4. Place a brown 8½" square on top of a multicolored block A, right sides together. Sew on the marked line. Trim seam allowances to ¼" and press toward the brown star point.

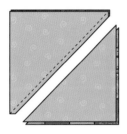

5. Repeat step 4 with three more of multicolored block A and four of block B. You will have a total of eight star points, four made with block A and four made with block B.

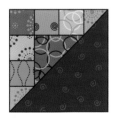
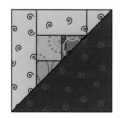

Make 4
with block A.

Make 4
with block B.

ASSEMBLING THE QUILT TOP

1. Following the diagram below, assemble the center of the quilt top, alternating block A and block B and positioning the brown blocks and eight star points as shown. Sew the blocks into rows, pressing seam allowances toward block B. Sew the rows together.

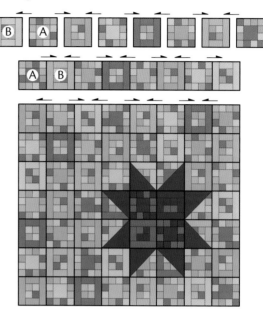

2. Sew the brown-with-green strips together end to end to create one continuous strip. From that long strip, cut two strips 2½" x 72½" and sew them to each side of the quilt top. Cut two strips 2½" x 68½" and sew them to the top and bottom of the quilt top. Press all seam allowances toward the border strips.

3. Sew 10 brown-with-green 4½" squares and 9 assorted 4½" squares together, alternating the brown squares with the assorted squares as shown. Press seam allowances toward the brown squares. Make 2 for the pieced side borders.

Pieced side border.
Make 2.

4. Sew the pieced side borders to each side of the quilt, pressing seam allowances toward the inner border.

5. To piece the top and bottom borders, sew 9 brown and 10 assorted 4½" squares together, alternating the assorted squares with the brown squares as shown. Press seam allowances toward the brown squares. Make 2.

Pieced top/bottom border.
Make 2.

6. Sew the pieced top and bottom borders to the quilt, pressing seam allowances toward the brown borders.

7. From the long brown-with-green strip from step 2, cut two strips 2½" x 84½". Sew a strip to each side of the quilt. From the remaining long strip, cut two strips 2½" x 80½", and sew them to the top and bottom of the quilt. Press seam allowances toward the brown border strips.

FINISHING THE QUILT

1. Mark your quilt for quilting if desired. Layer the top with batting and backing; baste.

2. Hand or machine quilt as desired. Our talented friend Karen Young quilted a continuous swirl design in the blocks and a wandering crosshatch in the star and borders.

3. Add a hanging sleeve if you intend to hang your quilt.

4. Cut the remaining assorted 2½"-wide strips into lengths ranging from 10" to 20" and sew them end to end to make one continuous strip. Bind your quilt with this strip, referring to "Straight-Grain Binding" on page 11 as needed.

5. Label your quilt.

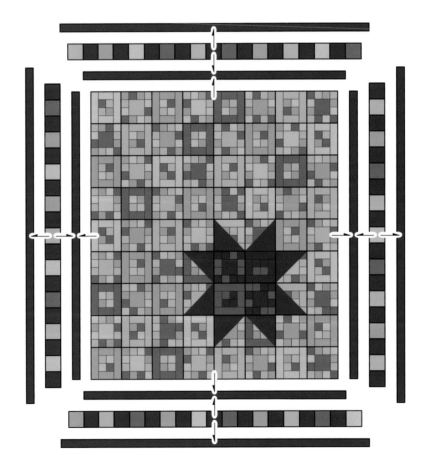

OPSCOTCH HINT ▸ PIECED BORDERS THAT FIT

Pieced borders sometimes require additional TLC, as they need to fit the quilt top in a precise manner. Pin the center of the border strip to the center edge of the quilt. Match the two ends and pin again. Then pin the remaining lengths of the border to the quilt. Gently ease the border in if it's a bit larger than the quilt or, if the quilt is a bit larger than the border, gently stretch the border to fit.

If your pieced border is too long or too short to ease in, either snug up your seam allowances by stitching just inside your seams, or take out a few seams and stitch with a slightly narrower seam allowance.

If your measurements are way off, and the pieces you are working with are fairly small, you can sometimes delete or add a piece to the pieced border (see "Starry Nights" on page 62). For Peppermint and Chocolate, adding or subtracting pieces isn't an option, because you will lose the pattern of alternating brown and colored squares.

Shining Plaids

Heather loves to work in plaids, and this great wall hanging was assembled completely from her stash, which she admits is rather healthy. She loves to have all of the lines of her plaids running straight (one of her perfectionist quilter issues), which requires a little more time when cutting but produces fabulous results. Using only medium to dark plaids in the blocks and borders allows the star to shine.

Pieced by Heather and hand quilted by Chloe and Corrine Collin

Finished quilt: 34½" x 34½"
Finished block: 4" x 4"
Skill level:

MATERIALS

Yardage is based on 42"-wide fabric.

1 yard total *or* 34 strips, 1½" x 20", of assorted medium to dark red, green, and blue plaids for blocks

⅝ yard of dark multicolored striped fabric for outer border

⅜ yard of assorted gold plaids for star

¼ yard of green plaid for inner border

½ yard of red plaid for binding

1⅓ yards for backing

40" x 40" piece of batting

CUTTING

All measurements include ¼" seam allowances.

From the assorted medium to dark red, green, and blue plaids, cut:

34 *total* strips, 1½" x 20"; from 12 of the strips cut:
  32 rectangles 1½" x 2½"
  32 rectangles 1½" x 4½"

2 strips, 2½" x 20"; cut into 16 squares 2½" x 2½"

From the assorted gold plaids, cut:

32 squares, 1½" x 1½"

4 rectangles, 1½" x 2½"

4 rectangles, 1½" x 4½"

2 squares, 2½" x 2½"

8 squares, 4½" x 4½"

From the green plaid, cut:

3 strips, 1½" x 42"

From the dark multicolored striped fabric, cut:

4 strips, 4½" x 42"

From the red plaid, cut:

2½"-wide bias strips, enough to yield 140"

CREATING THE BLOCKS

1. Sew two 1½" x 20" plaid strips together along the length of the strip. Repeat to make a total of five strip sets. Press seam allowances toward the darker of the two fabrics. Cut 13 units, 1½" wide, from each strip set to yield 65 two-square units. You will use only 64.

1½"

Make 5 strip sets.
Cut 65 units.

2. Sew four 1½" x 20" plaid strips together along the length of the strips. Repeat, using different color combinations, to make a total of three strip sets. Press all of the seam allowances in one direction. Cut the strip sets into 32 units, 1½" wide.

1½"

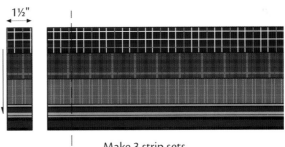

Make 3 strip sets.
Cut 32 units.

3. Following "Creating Block A" on page 31 from Peppermint and Chocolate, make 16 of block A.

4. Following "Creating Block B" on page 32, make 16 of block B.

5. In the same manner as "Creating the Star" on page 32, make two gold of block A and two gold of block B.

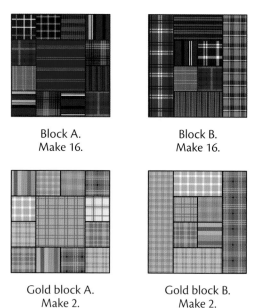

Block A.
Make 16.

Block B.
Make 16.

Gold block A.
Make 2.

Gold block B.
Make 2.

6. Using the eight 4½" gold squares, four of block A from step 3, and four of block B from step 4, follow the Peppermint and Chocolate instructions, steps 3 and 4 from "Creating the Star" to make the eight star points.

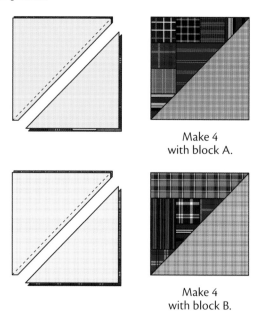

Make 4
with block A.

Make 4
with block B.

ASSEMBLING THE QUILT TOP

1. Arrange the blocks into six rows of six blocks each, alternating blocks A and B and placing the star blocks as shown. Sew the blocks into rows, pressing seam allowances toward block B. Sew the rows together. Press.

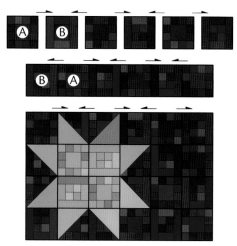

2. Sew the 1½"-wide green plaid strips end to end to make a continuous strip. From this long strip, cut two 1½" x 24½" inner-border strips. Sew them to the top and bottom of the quilt top. Press seam allowances toward the strips.

3. Cut two 1½" x 26½" strips from the green plaid strip. Sew them to the sides of the quilt. Press seam allowances toward the strips.

4. Trim the four dark multicolored striped strips to 4½" x 39½". Following the directions for "Mitered Borders" at right, sew the four strips to the quilt.

FINISHING THE QUILT

1. Mark your quilt for quilting if desired. Layer the top with batting and backing; baste.

2. Hand or machine quilt as desired. Our friends Chloe and Corinne Collin hand quilted our wall quilt.

3. Add a hanging sleeve if you intend to hang your quilt.

4. Using the 2½"-wide red plaid bias strips and referring to "Bias Binding" on page 12 as needed, sew the binding to the quilt.

5. Label your quilt.

MITERED BORDERS

We turn to mitered corners whenever we're working with striped fabric for our borders. This allows the stripe lines to merge into the corners of the border, rather than heading in two different directions.

1. Center the border strip along the side of the quilt so the same amount of border extends from each end. Stitch the border to the quilt, starting and stopping ¼" in from the ends of the quilt. Sew all four borders in place. Press seam allowances toward borders.

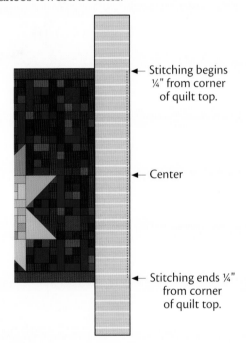

← Stitching begins ¼" from corner of quilt top.

← Center

← Stitching ends ¼" from corner of quilt top.

2. Working with one corner at a time, lay the quilt on a flat surface with the right side of the quilt top facing you. Lay one border piece on top of the other. Turn the top border piece under at a 45° angle, keeping the border strips running perpendicular to each other. Press in place.

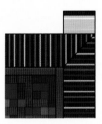

3. Place a piece of masking tape or painters' tape over the seam to hold it in place. Flip the quilt over diagonally and on the wrong side of the border, stitch along the pressed seam line. Start stitching at the inside corner, and stitch toward the outer edge of the border strips. We always stitch a scant ¹⁄₁₆" away from the pressed line in order to avoid sewing the tape into our border.

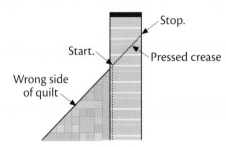

Stop.

Start.

Pressed crease

Wrong side of quilt

4. Remove the tape and press. Trim the seam allowance to ¼". Repeat for the remaining three corners.

HOPSCOTCH HINT ▷ **USING PLAIDS AND STRIPED FABRICS FOR QUILTING**

If you cut your plaid and striped fabrics along the woven lines, you can use the lines of the plaids and stripes as stitching lines. For the outer border of Shining Plaids, we quilted in ½" intervals using the stripes as our stitching guide. The trick is to cut and sew your plaids and striped fabrics straight!

Japanese Train Tiles

While traveling in Japan several years ago, Heather and Elissa noticed an amazing tile pattern on the floor of the bullet train they were riding. Elissa quickly sketched the design and they've been waiting for the perfect fabric to make it into a quilt. Although the quilt looks difficult, it's quick and easy to piece because it consists of two simple blocks. That being said, Heather happily sewed all her blocks together without realizing she had reversed the layout of some of the blocks by mistake. She also placed one block in her quilt sideways when sewing the blocks together. Heather happily sent the quilt off to Martingale, and it was Robin, the editor, who noticed the mistakes! Amazingly, neither of these errors is noticeable without a close look! Both the lap quilt and the place mats on page 44 are great projects for using fabrics from your stash.

Finished quilt: 58½" x 58½"
Finished blocks: 8" x 8"
Skill level:

MATERIALS

Yardage is based on 42"-wide fabric.

⅞ yard of blue print for outer border

⅓ yard *each* of 12 assorted blue, green, and pink prints for blocks*

⅓ yard *total* of assorted pink prints for inner border

¾ yard of blue plaid for binding

3¾ yards of backing

64" x 64" of batting

If you are using assorted scraps to make this quilt, substitute them for yardage in the cutting list.

CUTTING

All measurements include ¼" seam allowances.

From the assorted blue, green, and pink prints, cut a *total* of:

6 strips, 6½" x 21"
18 squares, 4½" x 4½"
36 rectangles, 2½" x 4½"
52 strips, 2½" x 21"

From the assorted pink prints for inner border, cut:

12 strips, 1½" x 21"

From the blue print, cut:

6 strips, 4½" x 42"

From the blue plaid, cut:

2½"-wide bias strips, enough to yield 240"

Pieced by Heather and quilted by Elissa

CREATING BLOCK A

1. Sew four assorted 2½" x 21" strips together along the length of the strips to create a strip set. Press seam allowances in one direction. Repeat to create five more strip sets. To create variety, use a different combination of fabrics to make each set. Cut the strip sets into 2½"-wide units. You need a total of 36 units for Block A.

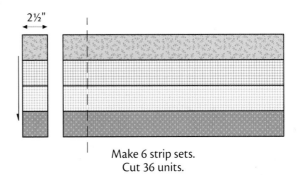

Make 6 strip sets.
Cut 36 units.

2. Sew two assorted 2½" x 21" strips together along the length of the strips to create a strip set. Press seam allowances toward the darker fabric. Repeat to make 10 more strip sets. Again, create diverse strip sets by using different fabric combinations. Cut the strip sets into 72 units, 2½" wide; 36 for block A and 36 for block B.

2½"

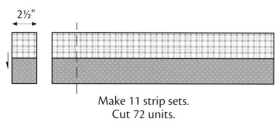

Make 11 strip sets.
Cut 72 units.

3. Sew a 2½" x 4½" rectangle to the end of a unit from step 2. Press the seam allowances toward the rectangle. Make 36.

Make 36.

4. Arrange two units from step 1 and two units from step 3, being careful that units with the same fabric do not lie next to each other. Sew the units together to make 10 of block A. Flip the position of the units from step 3 as shown to make a mirror image of block A. Make eight of block A reversed. Press the seam allowances toward the center of the blocks.

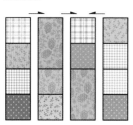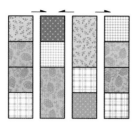

Block A.
Make 10.

Block A reversed.
Make 8.

CREATING BLOCK B

1. Sew a 2½" x 21" strip and a 6½" x 21" strip together along the length of the strips. Repeat with different fabrics to create 5 more strip sets. Each strip set should have a different combination of fabrics. Cut the strip sets into 36 units, 2½" wide.

2½"

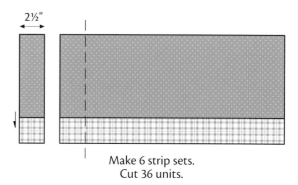

Make 6 strip sets.
Cut 36 units.

2. Sew two-square units from step 2 of "Creating Block A" on page 41 to opposite sides of a 4½" square. Press the seam allowances toward the center square. Make 18.

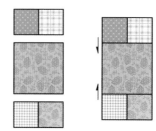

3. Arrange two units from step 1 and one unit from step 2 as shown, being careful units with the same fabric do not lie next to each other. Sew the units together to make 15 of block B. Flip the position of the units as shown to make a mirror image of block B. Make 3 of block B reversed. Press the seam allowances toward the outer strips.

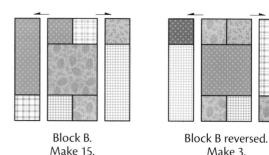

Block B.
Make 15.

Block B reversed.
Make 3.

ASSEMBLING THE QUILT TOP

1. Sew the blocks into six rows with six blocks in each row, alternating block A and block B as shown. Press seam allowances in alternate directions from row to row.

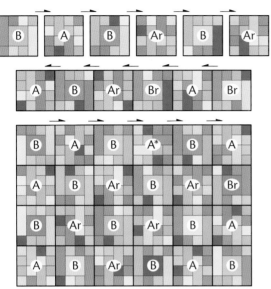

* Indicates rotated block.

2. Sew the assorted pink 1½"-wide strips together end to end to make a continuous strip. From that strip, cut two strips 1½" x 48½" long and sew them to the sides of the quilt. Press seam allowances toward the pink strips. Cut two strips 1½" x 50½" long and sew them to the top and bottom of the quilt. Press seam allowances toward the strips.

3. Sew the blue 4½"-wide strips together end to end to make a continuous strip. Cut two strips 4½" x 50½" and sew them to the sides of the quilt. Press seam allowances toward the blue strips. Cut two strips 4½" x 58½" and sew them to the top and bottom of the quilt. Press seam allowances toward the blue strips.

FINISHING THE QUILT

1. If necessary, mark your quilt for quilting. Layer the top with batting and backing; baste.

2. Hand or machine quilt as desired. Elissa quilted a continuous daisies-and-butterflies design on our long-arm quilting machine.

3. Add a hanging sleeve if you plan on hanging your quilt.

4. Using the plaid 2½"-wide bias strips and referring to "Bias Binding" on page 12 as needed, sew the binding to the quilt.

5. Label your quilt.

QUEEN-SIZE QUILT

Finished quilt: 82½" x 92½"

Finished blocks: 10" x 10"

Skill level:

We find ourselves returning to this pattern whenever we purchase new fabric bundles, since it's quick and easy to make and works well with a variety of print scales. Altering the size and number of blocks makes this pattern suitable for projects as small as place mats and as large as a king-size quilt! We created this queen-size quilt using floral fabrics and chose to feature a large-scale print in the center squares and border. We had fun making a large bed quilt out of totally different fabrics than we used in "Japanese Train Tiles" (page 40) and "Daisy Tile Place Mats" (page 44). For the queen-size quilt's materials list and instructions go to www.martingale-pub.com/extras/traintiles; then follow the assembly instructions for "Japanese Train Tiles."

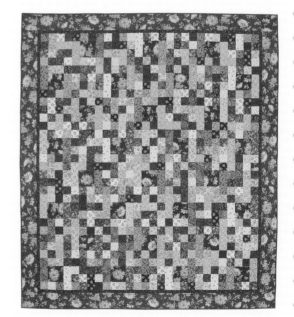

Daisy Tile Place Mats

This pattern lends itself to featuring a larger print in the plain center blocks. Elissa opted for a great daisy pri[nt] and then chose coordinating batiks for the rest of the blocks. The place mats are quick to create and make[s] great gift for a birthday or bridal shower.

Pieced and quilted by Elissa

Finished place mat: 14½" x 18½"
Finished blocks: 6" x 6"
Skill level: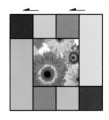

MATERIALS

Yardage is based on 42"-wide fabric and is enough for two place mats.

⅝ yard *total* of assorted orange, yellow, and pink batiks for blocks
⅜ yard of daisy print for blocks and borders
⅜ yard of pink batik for binding
¾ yard for backing
23" x 37" of batting

CUTTING

All measurements include ¼" seam allowances. Cutting and piecing instructions are for two place mats.

From the assorted orange, yellow, and pink batiks, cut:

72 squares, 2" x 2"
8 rectangles, 2" x 3½"
8 rectangles, 2" x 5"

From the daisy print, cut:

2 strips, 3½" x 42"; from *each* strip cut:
    2 squares, 3½" x 3½" (4 total)
    2 strips, 3½" x 14½" (4 total)
2 strips, 1½" x 42"; cut into 4 strips, 1½" x 12½"

From the pink batik, cut:

4 strips, 2½" x 42"

PIECING THE PLACE MATS

1. To make block A, arrange twelve 2" squares and two 2" x 3½" rectangles as shown. Sew pieces into rows and press as indicated. Sew rows together and press. Make 4 of block A.

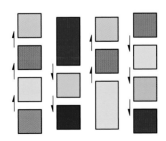 

Block A.
Make 4.

2. To make block B, arrange six 2" squares, two 2" x 5" rectangles, and one 3½" square as shown.

Sew pieces into rows and press as indicated. Sew rows together and press. Make four of block B.

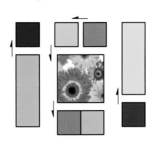

Block B.
Make 4.

3. Arrange two of block A, two of block B, two 1½" x 12½" daisy strips and two 3½" x 14½" daisy strips, following the illustration below. Sew the four blocks together to create the center of the place mat. Sew the 1½" x 12½" strips to the top and the bottom of the place-mat center. Press seam allowances toward the strips. Sew a 3½" x 14½" strip to each side of the place mat. Press seam allowances toward the strips. Make two place mats.

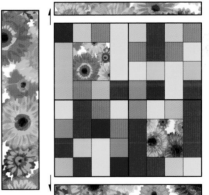 

FINISHING THE PLACE MATS

1. If needed, mark your place mat for quilting. Layer the place mat with batting and backing; baste.

2. Hand or machine quilt as desired. Elissa quilted ¼" away from the seam on the blocks and ½" apart along the sides of the place mat.

3. Using the 2½"-wide pink strips and referring to "Straight-Grain Binding" on page 11 as needed, bind your place mats.

Dippin' Dots Bag

This funky grommet bag is quick and easy to put together. Dig into your button jar, choose three coordinating fabrics, and you're on your way to a unique summer bag. An excellent gift for kids and teens!

Pieced, appliquéd, and quilted by Elissa

Finished bag: 13" x 18" (not including handles)

Skill level: ▦

MATERIALS

Yardage is based on 42"-wide fabric.

1 yard of green print for handles and lining

⅝ yard muslin*

⅜ yard of cream print for center panel

¼ yard of pink polka-dot print for side panels

4" x 8" pieces *each* of green, pink, and blue felted wool

19" x 41" piece of batting

8 silver grommets, 1⅝" diameter with 1" opening

6 pink, 5 green, and 4 blue ½" and ⅝" buttons

#8 pearl cotton in blue, green, and pink

Freezer paper

If your muslin doesn't measure at least 41" or wider, you'll need 1⅓ yards

CUTTING

All measurements include ¼" seam allowances.

From the cream print, cut:
1 rectangle, 10½" x 36½"

From the pink polka-dot print, cut:
2 strips, 2½" x 36½"

From the muslin, cut:
1 rectangle, 19" x 41"

From the green print, cut:
2 strips, 4½" x 42"

CREATING THE TOP

1. Sew a pink strip to each long edge of the cream rectangle. Press seam allowances toward the pink fabric. Your top should measure 14½" x 36½".

2. Layer the batting between the top and the muslin with the top right side up. Baste and quilt as desired. Elissa quilted a continuous swirl pattern on her bag. Trim batting and muslin even with the top.

3. Using the "Freezer-Paper Appliqué for Wool" method on page 9 and the patterns on page 49, cut the wool circles for the polka-dot appliqués. We

used three small, two medium, and one large pink circle; four small, two medium, and one large blue circle; and three small, one medium, and two large green circles. Arrange the circles on the cream print, layering a small circle on top of each large circle as shown. To leave room for the grommets, place circles at least 4½" from each edge that will be the bag top. Leave 1½" in the center free of circles, as that's where the fold at the bottom of the bag will be.

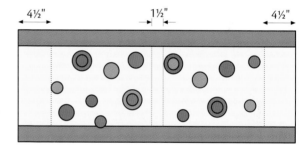

4. Use a blanket stitch (page 9) and coordinating colors of pearl cotton to appliqué the circles on the quilted panel.

5. Sew a button to the center of each circle using a coordinating color of pearl cotton.

PUTTING IT ALL TOGETHER

1. Measure the quilted panel. (Due to the quilting, it will be smaller than when you pinned the layers together.) Cut a piece of lining to the size of the quilted panel.

2. Place the lining on top of the quilted panel, right sides together. Stitch along the short sides of the bag. The long sides of the bag remain unstitched.

3. Fold the bag so the quilted front and back of the bag are right sides together and the lining is right sides together. On one side, stitch the length of the bag, backstitching when you begin and end stitching. On the opposite side, stitch along the quilted bag, and 8" into the lining, backstitching when you start and end. Leave an opening, and then stitch the remaining 4" of the seam.

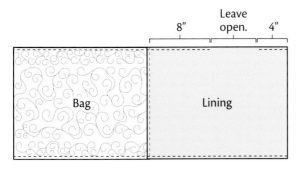

4. Turn the bag right side out. Fold the lining inside the bag and press along the top. Topstitch ¼" from the top edge to hold the lining in place.

5. Hand or machine stitch the opening on the side of the lining closed.

6. Mark the center of the grommet placement with dots 1½" from the top edge of the bag. The centers of the side-panel grommets are ½" from the edge of the pink panel. (The grommets will just edge into the cream panel.) On the front and back of the bag, mark the grommet centers 1¼" from the

edge of the pink panel. Of course you are welcome to move the grommets around to a position that pleases you. Following the manufacturer's instructions, attach the grommets to the top of the bag.

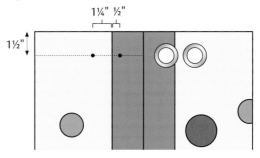

7. Sew the green print strips end to end to make a continuous strip.

8. Fold the strip right sides together along its length and stitch ¼" along the length of the strip. Turn right side out. Iron the strip flat.

9. Thread the handle through the grommets. If you prefer shorter handles on your bag, trim the strip to the desired length. On one end of the handle, turn ¼" of the raw edge to the inside of the handle and press. To join the handles into a loop, place the unturned end of the handle inside the turned end. Stitch across the edge of the fold.

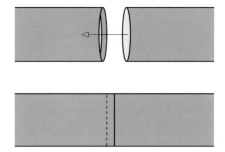

HOPSCOTCH HINT ▶ **GROMMETS IN A SNAP!**

The grommets Elissa used for this simple bag are literally a snap to use! No extra tools are required, and by applying the right amount of pressure, you can snap the grommets together by hand. Be careful to follow the manufacturer's instructions on the grommet package for assembly. Because you're working with multiple layers and bulky batting, you may need to cut the circles slightly larger than the given template for the grommets to fit. Begin by cutting your circles the size of the template and fit the grommets in place. If the circle is too snug for the grommet, carefully trim the circle ¹/₁₆" larger; then fit the grommets in place again.

Felted wool patterns do not require seam allowances. Add ¼" seam allowances for needle-turn appliqué.

Large
2½" diameter

Medium
2" diameter

Small
1½" diameter

Classic Tote

Elissa's bag is funky and fun, but as a teacher, Heather considers a bag a working part of her life. If it can't hol[d] a binder, a clipboard, and several books, Heather just doesn't consider it useful. This roomy tote is perfect fo[r] carrying any number of items, and it's fashionable to boot!

  Pieced, appliquéd, and quilted by Heather

Finished bag: 17" x 18" (not including handles)
Skill level:

MATERIALS

Yardage is based on 42"-wide fabric.

⅞ yard of dark batik for handles and lining

⅝ yard *total* of assorted dark batiks for bag (must be at least 40" wide)

¼ yard of cream batik for bag

Assorted scraps totaling 3" x 30" for circles

1⅜ yards of muslin*

32" x 45" piece of batting

8 metal buttons, assorted sizes

Freezer paper (optional)

If your muslin is 44" or wider, you only need ⅞ yard.

CUTTING

All measurements include ¼" seam allowances.

From the assorted dark batiks, cut:
4 strips, 2½" x 38½"
4 rectangles, 2½" x 19½"
2 strips, 2" x 38½"

From the cream batik, cut:
2 rectangles, 4½" x 19½"

From the muslin, cut:
1 rectangle, 26" x 45"

From the dark batik for handles and lining, cut:
2 strips 2½" x 42", cut into 4 rectangles, 2½" x 16"

From the batting, cut:
1 rectangle, 26" x 45"
2 rectangles, 2½" x 16"

CREATING THE TOP

1. From the assorted dark batiks and the cream batik, piece the top following the illustration below. Press seam allowances in one direction.

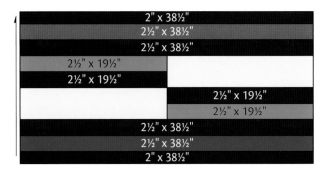

2. Using the appliqué method of your choice (refer to "Appliqué Methods" on page 8), and the patterns on page 49, prepare eight circles for appliqué.

We chose to appliqué two large circles, one small circle, and one medium circle to each cream rectangle. To add visual interest, on one side of the bag we appliquéd a small ninth circle on top of one of the large circles. Space the circles evenly along the cream rectangle. Do not appliqué any circles in the bottom 1½" of either rectangle, as this will become the base of the bag. Appliqué the circles in place.

3. Layer the batting between the bag top and the muslin with the top right side up. Baste and quilt as desired. We quilted in the ditch along each strip, as well as ¼" along one side of each strip's seam. Although you are not able to see the quilting in the ditch, this secures the layers (and helps in making the bottom corners of the bag later on). Trim the batting and muslin even with the bag top.

4. Sew a button to the center of each circle.

BUTTONS THAT STAY PUT

The only thing worse than losing a button is having to sew it back on when you find it. For buttons that stay put the first time, sew the button in place, turn the piece over and put a dab of Fray Check on the thread at the back of the button. Be careful to use just a small dab so that the Fray Check does not spread into the fabric and leave a mark. Once the Fray Check dries, that button will not be going anywhere the project isn't planning on going too!

PUTTING IT ALL TOGETHER

1. To make a handle, place two 2½" x 16" batik rectangles right sides together and place them on top of a 2½" x 16" batting rectangle. Sew with a ¼" seam allowance along each long side, leaving the short ends open. Turn right side out and press. Topstitch ¼" from the edge along each length of the rectangle. Repeat with the remaining 2½" x 16" batik and batting rectangles to make the second handle.

2. Measure the quilted piece. (Due to the quilting, it will be smaller than when you pinned the layers together.) Cut a piece of lining the size of the quilted piece.

3. Pin a handle on the right side of the bag with the raw edges of the handles along the short edges of the bag. Line up a corner of each handle with the seam of a batik strip. Pin the handles in place. When pinning the handles, make sure that each end of the handle extends ¼" beyond the edge of the bag and that they're directly opposite each other at each end of the bag. This will

allow the handle ends to be stitched into the final topstitching, making them more secure.

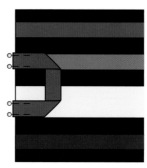

4. Place the lining on top of the quilted piece, right sides together. Stitch along the short sides of the bag using a generous ¼" seam allowance and stitching the handles into the seam. Re-stitch each seam to reinforce the handles and the bag top. The long sides of the bag are unstitched.

5. Fold the bag so the quilted front and back of the bag are right sides together and the lining is right sides together. On one side, stitch the length of the bag, backstitching when you begin and end stitching. On the opposite side, stitch along the quilted bag, and 8" into the lining, backstitching when you start and end. Leave an opening, and then stitch the remaining 4" of the seam.

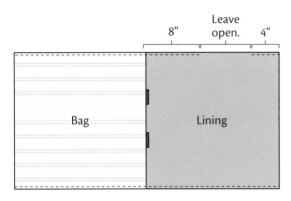

6. Before turning the bag, square up the bottom corners on both the bag and the lining. Fold each corner so the side seam of the bag runs from the point of the corner down the center of the triangle. To create side panels, stitch along the stitch-in-the-ditch quilting line that you created when quilting the bag. You will be sewing a line 2½" from the corner of the bag, creating a triangle. Repeat on the other side of the bag, and on both corners of the lining. Trim seam allowances to ¼".

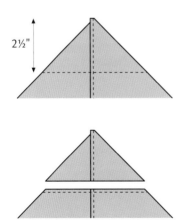

7. Turn the bag right side out. Hand or machine stitch the opening on the side of the lining closed. Fold the lining inside the bag and press along the top. Topstitch a scant ¼" from the top edge to hold the lining in place.

Circling the Patch

When you start cutting the fabric for this quilt, you'll probably ask yourself, "Why is there such a weird measurement for the center of the Nine Patch block?" When Heather and Elissa designed the quilt, they wanted a Nine Patch that was a little different. They drew several blocks, and this is the one they liked the best. It was all about appearances and nothing about the math!

Finished quilt: 59¼" x 71¾"

Finished block: 6¼" x 6¼"

Skill level:

MATERIALS

Yardage is based on 42"-wide fabric.

2⅓ yards of cream fabric for blocks

1⅔ yards *total* of assorted blue-and-red prints for blocks and circles

1½ yards of blue floral for border

⅝ yard of red floral for binding

½ yard of cream print for inner border

4 yards of backing fabric

65" x 78" of batting

Freezer paper (optional)

CUTTING

All measurements include ¼" seam allowances.

From the cream fabric, cut:

7 strips, 3¾" x 42"; cut into 128 rectangles, 2" x 3¾"

7 strips, 6¾" x 42"; cut into 31 squares, 6¾" x 6¾"

From the assorted blue-and-red prints, cut:

32 sets*:

1 square, 3¾" x 3¾" (32 total)

4 squares, 2" x 2" (128 total)

*All 5 squares in a set should be cut from the same fabric.

From the cream print, cut:

6 strips, 2" x 42"

From the blue floral, cut:

6 strips, 6½" x 42"

From the red floral, cut:

7 strips, 2½" x 42"

Pieced by Heather; quilted by Elissa and Heather

CREATING THE NINE PATCH BLOCKS

To create one Nine Patch block, use one 3¾" square and four 2" squares of the same red or blue print, and four 2" x 3¾" cream rectangles.

1. Sew cream rectangles to the top and bottom of the 3¾" square. Press seam allowances toward the center square.

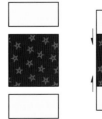

HOPSCOTCH HINT — AN UNCANNY RESEMBLANCE

If you're looking for perfect circles in different sizes, check out your pantry before you purchase templates. Tracing the bottom of a can will give you a perfectly round circle (assuming the edge isn't dented). The circles in this quilt come from tracing the bottom of a soup can, a kidney-bean can, and a stewed-tomatoes can. Not very scientific, but hey, it works!

2. Sew a 2" print square to each end of the remaining two cream rectangles. Press seam allowances toward the print squares.

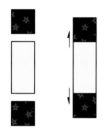

3. Sew the units from step 2 to the sides of the unit from step 1. Press seam allowances away from the center of the block.

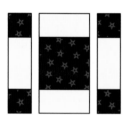 

Nine-Patch block.
Make 32.

4. Repeat steps 1–3 to create 32 Nine Patch blocks.

CREATING THE CIRCLE BLOCKS

1. Prepare 31 circles for appliqué using your favorite method. (For appliqué instructions refer to "Appliqué Methods" on page 8.) We used 8 large, 8 small, and 15 medium circles. The quilt would also look fabulous using circles that are all the same size.

2. Center each circle on a 6¾" cream square and appliqué in place. Make 31 Circle blocks.

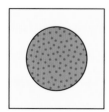

Circle block.
Make 31.

ASSEMBLING THE QUILT TOP

1. Arrange the blocks, following the diagram above right. Move the blocks around until you find a layout you like. Sew the blocks into rows, pressing seam allowances toward the circle blocks. Sew the rows together.

2. Sew the cream print strips together end to end to create a continuous strip. Measure the quilt through the center from top to bottom and cut two strips to that measurement. Sew the strips to the sides of the quilt. Press seam allowances toward the border strips.

3. Measure the quilt from side to side, including the border strips you just added. Cut two strips from the remainder of the long strip to that measurement. Sew them to the top and bottom of the quilt. Press seam allowances toward the border strips.

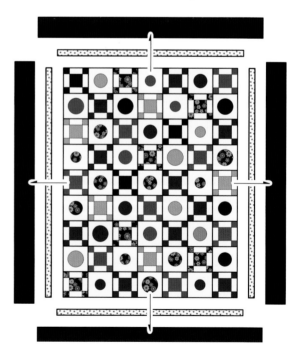

4. Repeat steps 2 and 3 with the blue 6½"-wide strips.

CREATING UNIQUE LABELS

While we firmly believe in labeling every quilt, it can sometimes be difficult to find great labels to purchase. Although it takes a little more time, you can often create unique labels using your quilt as an inspiration. Heather made her label for "Circling the Patch" by using the circle motif from the front of the quilt. It didn't take a lot of time, and it adds to the personality of the quilt.

FINISHING THE QUILT

1. Mark your quilt for quilting as desired. Layer the top with batting and backing; baste.

2. Hand or machine quilt as desired. Elissa quilted flowers in the outer borders, daisies in the circles, and loops in the cream of the blocks and inner border using her long-arm quilting machine. Heather then quilted diagonal lines through the Nine Patch blocks using her sewing machine.

3. Add a hanging sleeve if you intend to hang your quilt.

4. Using the 2½"-wide red floral strips and referring to "Straight-Grain Binding" on page 11 as needed, bind your quilt.

5. Label your quilt.

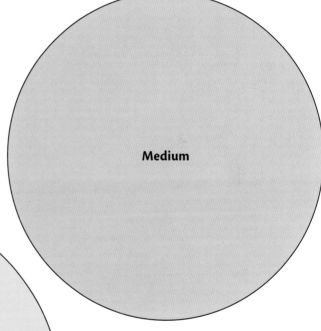

Medium

Large

Small

Patterns do not include
seam allowances.
Add ¼" seam allowances
for needle-turn appliqué.

Polka-Dot Party

This fun quilt works well with scraps as well as cut yardage. It's perfect for kids to wrap up in while in front of the TV, in the car, or while reading a great book.

Finished quilt: 45½" x 64"
Finished block: 3" x 3"
Skill level:

MATERIALS

Yardage is based on 42"-wide fabric.

2⅞ yards black-with-dot fabric for blocks and
    top panel
1⅔ yards *total* of assorted yellow, blue, pink, green,
    orange, and purple prints for blocks and binding
½ yard of assorted colored prints for circles
3¼ yards of backing
52" x 75" of batting
Freezer paper (optional)

CUTTING

All measurements include ¼" seam allowances.

From the black-with-dot fabric, cut from the
lengthwise grain:
1 piece, 13" x 46"
7 strips, 3½" x 46"; crosscut strips into 91 squares,
    3½" x 3½"

From the remaining black-with-dot fabric, cut from
the *crosswise* grain:
3 strips, 3½" x 42"; crosscut into 36 squares,
    3½" x 3½" (127 total 3½" squares)
20 strips, 1½" x 42"

From the assorted yellow, blue, pink, green,
orange, and purple prints, cut a *total* of:
25 strips, 1½" x 42"
7 strips, 2½" x 42"

Pieced and quilted by Elissa; hand appliquéd by Heather

CREATING THE BLOCKS

The Nine Patch blocks can be made quickly by
strip piecing.

1. Sew a black 1½"-wide strip on either side of a
colored 1½"-wide strip, sewing along the length of
the strips. Press seam allowances toward the black.
Repeat using different colors for the center strips to
create four more strip sets. Cut the strip sets into
1½"-wide units. Cut 128 units.

1½"

Make 5 strip sets.
Cut 128 units.

2. Sew two different colored 1½"-wide strips on either side of a black 1½"-wide strip, sewing along the length of the strips. Press seam allowances toward the black. Repeat using different color combinations to create 9 more strip sets. Cut the strip sets into 1½"-wide units. Cut 256 units.

1½"

Make 10 strip sets.
Cut 256 units.

3. Sew a unit from step 2 on either side of a unit from step 1 to create a Nine Patch block. Press. Make 128 blocks.

Nine-Patch block.
Make 128.

APPLIQUÉING THE CIRCLE PANEL

Refer to "Appliqué Methods" on page 8 as needed.

1. Using your favorite method of appliqué and the patterns on page 57, prepare 16 circles to be appliquéd on the top panel. We used 4 large, 6 medium and 6 small circles. You may choose to change the amounts or the sizes of the circles to create your own unique circle panel.

2. Arrange the circles on the black 13" x 46" panel, overlapping some of the circles and leaving others to "float" on their own. Be sure to leave 1" of space all around the edges of the panel to allow for trimming and the seam allowances.

3. Appliqué the circles in place.

4. Trim the panel to 12½" x 45½".

CREATING THE QUILT TOP

Following the diagram below, sew the blocks and 3½" squares into rows. Press seam allowances toward the plain squares. Sew the rows together to make the pieced section of the quilt top. Sew the circle panel to the top of the quilt. Press seam allowances toward the panel.

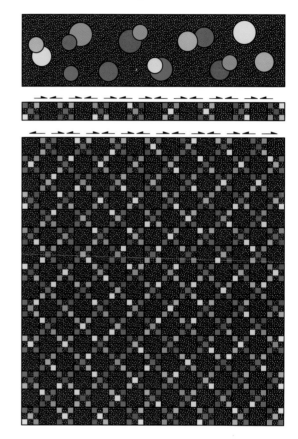

FINISHING THE QUILT

1. If necessary, mark your quilt for quilting. Layer the top with batting and backing; baste.

2. Hand or machine quilt as desired. Elissa quilted a continuous loop pattern on the quilt top and swirls in each of the circles using her long-arm quilting machine.

3. Add a hanging sleeve if you intend to hang your quilt.

4. Cut the assorted 2½"-wide strips into lengths ranging from 12" to 18" and sew end to end to make one continuous strip at least 245" long. Use this strip to bind your quilt, referring to "Straight-Grain Binding" (page 11) as needed.

5. Label your quilt.

DIVING INTO THE SCRAP BAG

Heather created this adorable baby quilt by making the pieced section of Polka-Dot Party. She used the scraps from a leftover queen-size quilt she made for Elissa. The simple hand quilting results in a stunning quilt. Dive into your scrap bag to create your own classic, yet unique, quilt.

Finished size: 45½" x 57½". Pieced by Heather;
hand quilted by Corinne Collin and Gelane Ondrik.

Starry Nights

Elissa's love affair with Moda Marbles began when she and Heather opened Hopscotch Quilt Shop. They seem to sneak their way into many of her quilts. In this quilt, the pure solid colors against the black background make them pop and remind her of Skittles!

Finished quilt: 66½" x 66½"
Finished block: 10" x 10"
Skill level: ▦ ▦ ▦

MATERIALS

Yardage is based on 42"-wide fabric.

4½ yards of black Marble for background and binding

2 yards *total* of assorted bright orange, turquoise, blue, pink, green, yellow, and purple Marble for blocks and pieced border

¼ yard of lime green Marble for inner border

4¼ yards of backing

72" x 72" of batting

CUTTING

Cutting instructions are for one block only.
Measurements include ¼" seam allowances.

Sarah's Choice

From the black Marble, cut:

1 square, 6¼" x 6¼"; cut the square into quarters diagonally to yield 4 triangles

4 squares, 3" x 3"

From *one of the* assorted Marbles, cut:

4 squares, 3⅜" x 3⅜"; cut the squares in half diagonally to yield 8 triangles

From *a second* assorted Marble, cut:

4 squares, 3⅜" x 3⅜"; cut the squares in half diagonally to yield 8 triangles

X Quartet

From the black Marble, cut:

4 squares, 3" x 3"

4 squares, 3⅜" x 3⅜"; cut the squares in half diagonally to yield 8 triangles

2 rectangles, 3" x 5½"

Pieced and quilted by Elissa

From *one of the* assorted Marbles, cut:

4 squares, 3⅜" x 3⅜"; cut the squares in half diagonally to yield 8 triangles

Rising Star

From the black Marble, cut:

1 square, 6¼" x 6¼"; cut the square into quarters diagonally to yield 4 triangles

1 square, 3¾" x 3¾"; cut the square into quarters diagonally to yield 4 triangles

5 squares, 3" x 3"

4 squares, 1¾" x 1¾"

From *one of the* assorted Marbles, cut:

4 squares, 3⅜" x 3⅜"; cut the squares in half diagonally to yield 8 triangles

From *a second* assorted Marble, cut:

4 squares, 2⅛" x 2⅛"; cut the squares in half diagonally to yield 8 triangles

Crown and Star

From the black Marble, cut:

2 squares, 3¾" x 3¾"; cut the squares into quarters
   diagonally to yield 8 triangles
4 squares, 3" x 3"
4 squares, 2⅛" x 2⅛", cut the squares in half
   diagonally to yield 8 triangles
12 squares, 1¾" x 1¾"

From *one of the* assorted Marbles, cut:

1 square, 3" x 3"
4 squares, 2⅛" x 2⅛", cut the squares in half
   diagonally to yield 8 triangles

From a second assorted Marble, cut:

4 rectangles, 1¾" x 3"
8 squares, 2⅛" x 2⅛", cut the squares in half
   diagonally to yield 16 triangles

Crystal Star

From the black Marble, cut:

1 square, 6¼" x 6¼"; cut the square into quarters
   diagonally to yield 4 triangles
2 squares, 3⅜" x 3⅜"; cut the squares in half
   diagonally to yield 4 triangles
4 squares, 3" x 3"

From *one of the* assorted Marbles, cut:

1 square, 4" x 4"

From a second assorted Marble, cut:

4 squares, 3⅜" x 3⅜"; cut the squares in half
   diagonally to yield 8 triangles

Centennial

From the black Marble, cut:

1 square, 6¼" x 6¼"; cut the square into quarters
   diagonally to yield 4 triangles
4 squares, 3" x 3"

From *one of the* assorted Marbles, cut:

4 rectangles, 2¼" x 4"

From a second assorted Marble, cut:

2 squares, 3¾" x 3¾"; cut the square into quarters
   diagonally to yield 8 triangles
1 square, 4" x 4"

Sashing, Borders and Binding
From the black Marble, cut:

18 strips, 2" x 42"
5 strips, 4¼" x 42"; cut the strips into 40 squares,
   4¼" x 4¼". Cut the squares into quarters
   diagonally to yield 160 triangles.
1 strip, 2⅜" x 42"; cut into 8 squares, 2⅜" x 2⅜".
   Cut the squares in half diagonally to yield
   16 triangles.
7 strips, 2½" x 42"

From the lime green Marble, cut:

7 strips, 1" x 42"

From the assorted Marbles, cut:

6 strips, 2⅝" x 42"; crosscut into 84 squares,
   2⅝" x 2⅝"

CREATING THE BLOCKS
This quilt features six different block patterns. Elissa made four of each pattern, plus one extra X Quartet block for a total of 25 blocks. You can customize your quilt by making more or less of each block as desired. Refer to the Hopscotch Hint box "Location, Location, Location" on page 71 for tips on changing color placement to make each quilt block look unique.

Referring to the illustrations at right, arrange the pieces for each block. Sew the pieces into rows; then sew the rows together. Press the seam allowances in the direction of the pressing arrows.

Sarah's Choice

Sew the block together following the illustration below.

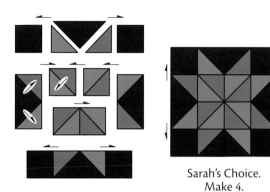

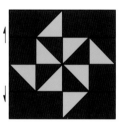

Sarah's Choice.
Make 4.

Crown and Star

Sew the block together following the illustration below.

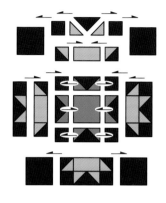

Crown and Star.
Make 4.

X Quartet

Sew the block together following the illustration below.

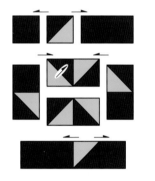

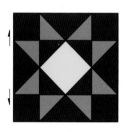

X Quartet.
Make 5.

Crystal Star

Sew the block together following the illustration below.

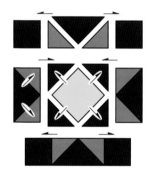

Crystal Star.
Make 4.

Rising Star

Sew the block together following the illustration below.

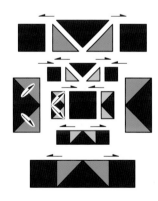

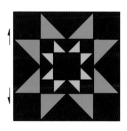

Rising Star.
Make 4.

Centennial

Sew the block together following the illustration below.

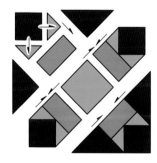

Centennial.
Make 4.

CREATING THE QUILT TOP

1. Sew the 2"-wide black marble strips together end to end to create one continuous strip. From this strip, cut twenty 2" x 10½" sashing strips. Arrange blocks in 5 rows, with 5 star blocks in each row. Refer to the diagram below. Sew a sashing strip between each star block, but do not sew a sashing strip on the ends of the rows. Press the seam allowances toward the black sashing strips.

2. From the continuous strip, cut 6 sashing strips 2" x 56½". Sew the rows together, sewing a sashing strip between each row. Add a sashing strip to the top and bottom of the quilt. Press the seam allowances toward the black sashing strips.

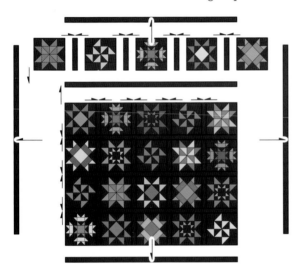

3. From the remainder of the long sashing strip, cut two strips 2" x 59½". Sew one to each side of the quilt, pressing the seam allowances toward the sashing strips.

4. Sew the lime green 1"-wide strips together end to end to create one continuous strip. Cut two strips 1" x 59½" and sew them to the top and bottom of the quilt. Press the seam allowances toward the lime green border strips.

5. From the remainder of the lime green strip, cut two strips 1" x 60½". Sew one to each side of the quilt. Press seam allowances toward the lime green border strips.

PIECING THE OUTER BORDER

1. To make a border unit, sew a large black triangle to the top-right and the bottom-left side of an assorted 2⅝" square as shown. Press the seam allowances toward the black fabric. Make 76 border units.

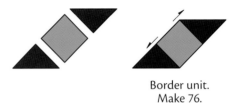

Border unit.
Make 76.

2. To make a corner unit, sew a small black triangle to the top and bottom on the right side of an assorted 2⅝" square as shown. Sew a large triangle to the lower-left side of the colored square. Make eight corner units.

Corner unit.
Make 8.

3. For the pieced top and bottom borders, sew 18 border units together as shown below to create a continuous strip. Sew a corner unit to each end of the strip. Make two. Sew them to the top and bottom of the quilt. Press the seam allowances toward the lime green border.

4. For the pieced side borders, sew 20 border units together end to end to create a continuous strip. Add a corner unit to each end of the strip. Make two. Sew one to each side of the quilt. Press the seam allowances toward the lime green border.

Top/bottom pieced border.
Make 2.

Side pieced border.
Make 2.

If you have difficulty getting your pieced borders to fit, refer to the Hopscotch Hint box "Pieced Borders That Fit" on page 35.

FINISHING THE QUILT

1. If necessary, mark your quilt for quilting. Layer the top with batting and backing; baste.

2. Hand or machine quilt as desired. Elissa quilted loops in each star, a continuous swirl-and-star pattern in the black Marble, and swirls in each of the colored diamonds using her long-arm quilting machine.

3. Add a hanging sleeve if you intend to hang your quilt.

4. Using the 2½"-wide black Marble strips and referring to "Straight-Grain Binding" on page 11 as needed, bind your quilt.

5. Label your quilt.

HOPSCOTCH HINT ▶ **PLAYING WITH QUILT BLOCKS**

If you enjoy creating different quilt blocks, we highly recommend Judy Hopkins' book *501 Rotary-Cut Quilt Blocks* (Martingale & Company, 2008). This amazing resource not only includes the cutting and piecing directions for 501 blocks, but it also shows how to make each block in six different sizes. We use this book so much that we took our copy to our local copy center and had it spiral bound. Now we can turn to any page and work with the book lying open flat. Spiral-binding your favorite quilt books is inexpensive and will save wear and tear on the book over time.

Stash of Stars

Except for the border, Heather was able to piece this king-size quilt entirely from her stash. Although the quilt is made with only two colors, its scrappy design allowed her to use many little leftover pieces that had been squirreled away among her red fabrics. One of the challenges of making a two-color quilt is balancing dark, medium, and light prints. While Heather had lots of dark red and tan prints, she had very few medium-value prints. This was a challenge, as many of the blocks needed a medium print in order to create the design.

Finished quilt: 95"¾ x 95"¾
Finished block: 10" x 10"
Skill level:

MATERIALS

Yardage is based on 42"-wide fabric.

4¾ yards of assorted tan prints for blocks, corner
   posts, and setting squares
4 yards of assorted red prints for blocks and sashing
3½ yards of red floral for inner and outer borders
   and binding
½ yard of tan print for middle border
9 yards of backing
100" x 100" of batting

CUTTING

All measurements include ¼" seam allowances.

From the assorted red prints, cut:
100 strips, 1½" x 10½"

From the assorted tan prints, cut:
60 squares, 1½" x 1½"
4 squares, 15¾" x 15¾"; cut each square into
   quarters diagonally to yield 16 setting triangles*
2 squares, 8" x 8"; cut the squares in half diagonally
   to yield 4 corner triangles

From the red floral, cut:
8 strips, 2" x 42"
10 strips, 6¾" x 42"
10 strips, 2½" x 42"

From the tan print for middle bordder, cut:
9 strips, 1½" x 42"

** If you don't have 15¾" squares, you can cut 8
squares, 11" x 11"; cut the squares in half diagonally
to yield 16 setting triangles. Care must be taken
when sewing and pressing these triangles, as the
bias edge of the triangles lie along the edge of the
quilt top and can easily stretch.*

CREATING THE BLOCKS

To make Stash of Stars you need a total of 41 blocks.
Heather used the same star blocks that Elissa used
in "Starry Nights" on page 62. Refer to "Cutting"
on pages 63 and 64 and "Creating the Blocks" on
pages 64 and 65 for instructions on making each
block. Heather made seven blocks each of Sarah's
Choice, Rising Star, Centennial Star, Crystal Star,
and Crown and Star, and six X Quartet blocks for
a total of 41 blocks. You can customize your quilt
by adjusting the number of blocks you make from
each block pattern.

Sarah's Choice (1).
Make 7.

X Quarter (2).
Make 6.

Rising Star (3).
Make 7.

Crown and Star (4).
Make 7.

Crystal Star (5).
Make 7.

Centennial (6).
Make 7.

Pieced by Heather and machine quilted by Karen Young

CREATING THE QUILT TOP

1. Following the diagram below, sew the quilt blocks and red 1½" x 10½" sashing strips together in diagonal rows. Press seam allowances toward the sashing strips.

2. Sew the sashing strips and tan squares together in rows, pressing the seam allowances toward the red sashing.

3. Sew the corresponding sashing row to the top of the appropriate pieced block row. Add setting triangles to each end. Sew the rows together and add corner triangles.

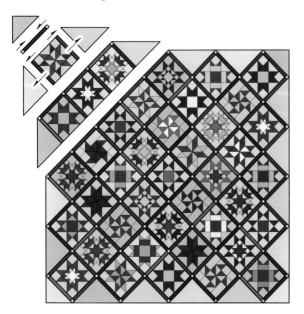

4. Trim the setting triangles ¼" from the point of the sashing and tan squares.

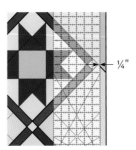

5. Sew the red 2"-wide inner-border strips together end to end to make a continuous strip. Measure the quilt top through the center from bottom to top and cut two strips to that measurement. Sew the strips to each side of the quilt. Press the seam allowances toward the red border strips.

6. Measure the quilt top through the center from side to side, including the borders added in step 5. Cut two strips from the remainder of the long strip to that measurement. Sew the strips to the top and bottom of the quilt. Press the seam allowances toward the border strips.

7. Repeat steps 5 and 6 to add the tan middle-border strips, and then the red 6¾"-wide outer-border strips.

FINISHING THE QUILT

1. If necessary, mark your quilt for quilting. Layer the top with batting and backing; baste.

2. Hand or machine quilt as desired. Elissa didn't want to tackle a king-size quilt, so our talented friend Karen Young quilted a continuous-line floral design using her long-arm quilting machine.

3. Add a hanging sleeve if you intend to hang your quilt.

4. Using the red 2½"-wide strips and referring to "Straight-Grain Binding" on page 11, bind your quilt.

5. Label your quilt.

HOPSCOTCH HINT ▶ **LOCATION, LOCATION, LOCATION**

While Stash of Stars looks like it's made up of many quilt block patterns, it's really only made up of six different blocks. Changing the location of the dark, medium, and light prints causes the blocks to take on an entirely new look. Examine the three blocks below. They're all Sarah's Choice, but at first glance, they look like three different pieced blocks.

Summer Warmth Table Topper

This quilt was originally going to have cotton appliqué, but when Heather stumbled across some amazing gold and turquoise hand-dyed wool (available from Sue Spargo), she couldn't resist. You could also create the quilt with a red, green, and gold center surrounded by red flowers to dress up your table for the Christmas season.

Finished quilt: 44½" x 44½"
Finished block: 6" x 6"
Skill level:

MATERIALS

Fat quarters measure 18" x 20". Other yardage is based on 42"-wide fabric.

1 fat quarter *each* of 3 yellow prints, 3 blue prints, and 3 green prints for blocks and binding

1 yard of brown print for outer border

20" x 20" *total* of assorted gold felted wool for flowers (We used 5 different shades.)

12" x 18" green felted wool for vines

12" x 12" *total* of assorted green felted wool for leaves (We used 4 different shades.)

7" x 7" *total* assorted blue felted wool for flower centers (We used 3 different shades.)

3 yards of backing fabric

50" x 50" of batting

Freezer Paper

3-strand embroidery floss in shades of gold, green, and turquoise

Size 5 gold pearl cotton

CUTTING

All measurements include ¼" seam allowances.

From *each* of the assorted yellow, blue, and green fat quarters, cut:

5 strips, 2" x 20" (45 total; you will only need 42)

Choose 4 assorted strips from each color group and cut these strips into:

 2 rectangles, 2" x 3½" (24 total)

 2 rectangles, 2" x 6½" (24 total)*

1 to 2 strips, 2½" x 20" (11 assorted strips in total)

From the brown print, cut:

4 strips, 7½" x 42"

From the green felted wool for vines, cut:

⅜"-wide bias strips, enough to yield 135"

If your fabric does not have 20" of usable width, cut the 2 larger rectangles and 1 of the smaller rectangles from the strip. Cut the remaining small rectangle from the remaining fabric in the same fat quarter.

Pieced and appliquéd by Heather; machine quilted by Elissa

CREATING THE SIXTEEN PATCH BLOCKS

1. Sew four assorted 2" x 20" strips together along their length to create a strip set. Repeat with different colors to make five more strips sets. (You'll have nine strips remaining.) Press seam allowances in the same direction. Cut strip sets into 2"-wide units to create 52 four-square units.

Make 6 strip sets.
Cut 52 units.

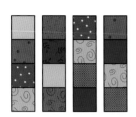

2. Sew the Sixteen Patch blocks together using four different four-square units. Make 13 blocks.

16 Patch block.
Make 13.

CREATING THE FOUR PATCH BLOCKS

1. Sew two assorted 2" x 20" strips together along the length of the strip. Make one strip set of each color combination (three total), following the illustration below. Cut the strip sets into 2"-wide units. You'll need eight units from each strip set (24 total).

2"
Make 1 strip set.
Cut 8 units.

2"
Make 1 strip set.
Cut 8 units.

2"
Make 1 strip set.
Cut 8 units.

2. Sew two units from the same strip set together to create a four-patch unit. Make four. Repeat with the remaining strip sets so you have four four-patch units from each color combination (12 total).

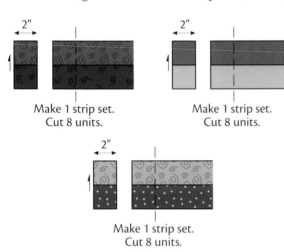

Four-patch unit.
Make 4 from each color combination.

3. The outer border of each Four Patch block will be made from the color that's not used in the four-patch unit. For example, a green-and-yellow four-patch unit will have a blue border. Sew a contrast-color 2" x 3½" rectangle to the top and bottom of a four-patch unit. Press the seam allowances toward the rectangles.

4. Sew a 2" x 6½" rectangle of the same fabric used in step 3 to each side of the block. Press the seam allowances toward the rectangles.

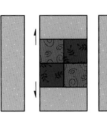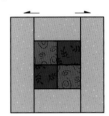

5. Repeat to make a total of 12 Four Patch blocks: 4 with green borders, 4 with yellow borders, and 4 with blue borders.

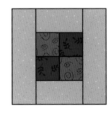

Four-patch block.
Make 4 from each color combination.

ASSEMBLING THE QUILT TOP

1. Arrange the blocks in five rows of five blocks each, alternating the Sixteen Patch blocks and the Four Patch blocks and referring to the diagram above right.

2. Sew the blocks into rows, pressing the seam allowances toward the Four Patch blocks. Sew the rows together to form the pieced center of the quilt.

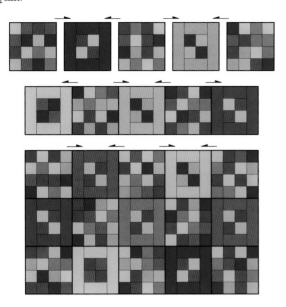

3. Sew the brown strips together end to end to make a continuous strip. From the long strip, cut two strips 7½" x 30½". Sew the cut strips to each side of the quilt and press the seam allowances toward the border strips.

4. From the remaining brown strip, cut two pieces 7½" x 44½" and sew them to the top and bottom of the quilt. Press the seam allowances toward the border strips.

APPLIQUÉING THE BORDER

The border is appliquéd using wool, but you could make your quilt with cotton appliqués. Referring to "Freezer-Paper Appliqué for Wool" on page 9, make templates for the large, medium, and small flowers, flower centers, and the leaves using the patterns on page 76.

1. Cut a total of 16 flowers. We used 5 large flowers, 8 medium flowers, and 3 small flowers. Lay the flowers on the borders in an arrangement that you like and pin them in place.

2. Arrange the green bias strips for the vines so that they flow from one flower to the next. Pin the vines in place.

3. Use a blanket stitch and coordinating 3-strand floss to sew the flowers and vines to the quilt top, referring to "Embroidery Stitches" on page 9 as needed.

4. Cut 27 leaves from assorted green wool. Arrange as desired; pin and blanket stitch in place. Repeat using the blue wool for the flower centers. We used round flower centers for the large and medium flowers, and oval flower centers for the small flowers.

5. To create texture in the flower centers, use the gold pearl cotton to make French knots.

FINISHING THE QUILT

1. If necessary, mark your quilt for quilting. Layer the top with batting and backing; baste.

2. Hand or machine quilt as desired. At Heather's suggestion, Elissa machine quilted a continuous pattern of leaves in the border of the quilt and flowers in the pieced center of the quilt using her long-arm quilting machine.

3. Sew the 11 assorted yellow, blue, and green 2½"-wide strips together end to end to create a continuous binding strip. Bind your quilt referring to "Straight-Grain Binding" on page 11 as needed.

4. Label your quilt and put it on the table to enjoy!

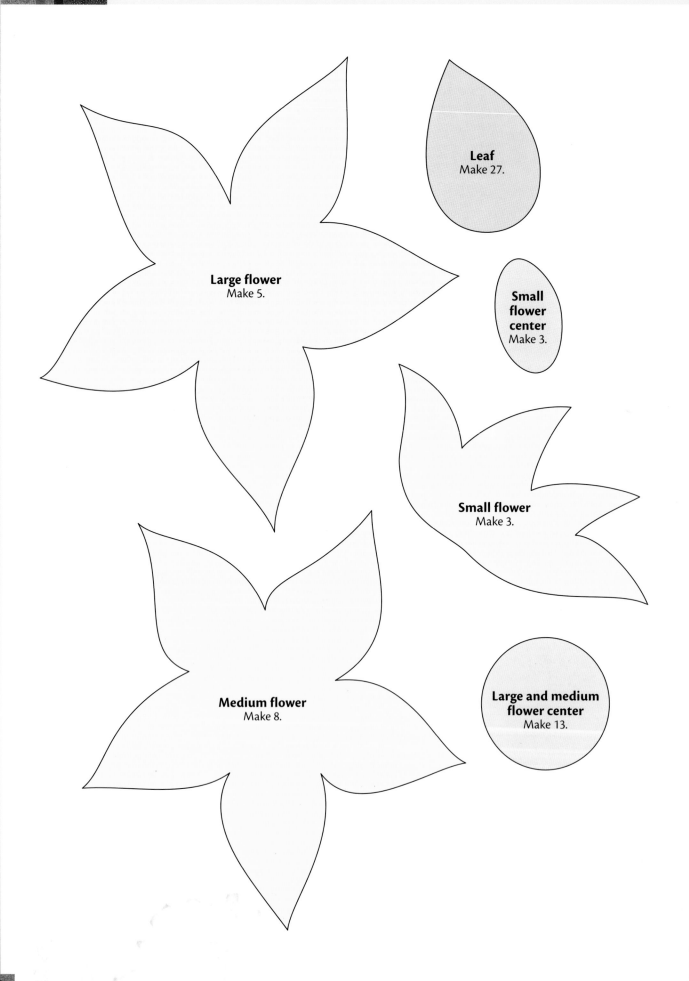

Leaf
Make 27.

Large flower
Make 5.

Small
flower
center
Make 3.

Small flower
Make 3.

Medium flower
Make 8.

Large and medium
flower center
Make 13.

Soaking Up the Sun

One cheery Jelly Roll plus fabric for borders and binding are all that is needed for this sunny lap quilt. Grab a glass of sun tea and enjoy creating this quick and easy weekend project.

Finished quilt: 48½" x 64½"
Finished block: 8" x 8"
Skill level: ■

MATERIALS

1 Jelly Roll (precut 2½" x 42" strips) containing 26 medium to dark strips and 14 light strips for blocks

OR

2 yards *total* of assorted medium and dark prints for blocks

1 yard *total* of assorted light prints for blocks

⅞ yard of green floral for outer border

½ yard of diagonally striped fabric for binding

3¼ yards for backing

54" x 70" piece of batting

CUTTING

All measurements include ¼" seam allowances.

If you're using yardage instead of precut Jelly Roll strips, cut 26 strips, 2½" x 42" from the assorted medium and dark prints. Cut 14 strips, 2½" x 42" from the assorted light strips.

From the assorted light prints, cut:
36 rectangles, 2½" x 4½"
36 rectangles, 2½" x 8½"

From the green floral, cut:
6 strips, 4½" x 42"

From the diagonally striped fabric, cut:
6 strips, 2½" x 42"

CREATING THE BLOCKS

If you're using a Jelly Roll, divide the roll into a group of 26 medium to dark strips and another group of 14 light strips.

Follow the instructions from the "Summer Warmth Table Topper" on pages 73 and 74 for piecing the blocks.

Pieced and quilted by Elissa

1. To make the Sixteen Patch blocks, use 20 assorted medium to dark strips and make 5 strip sets. Cut 68 units, 2½" wide. Make 17 Sixteen Patch blocks.

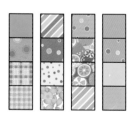 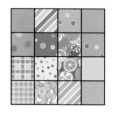

16-Patch block.
Make 17.

2. Using six assorted medium to dark print strips, make three strip sets. Cut them into 36 units 2½" wide. Unlike Summer Warmth, the center four-patch units are made from two different two-square units. Make 18 four-patch units.

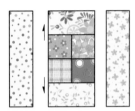

Make 18.

3. Use the assorted light 2½" x 4½" and 2½" x 8½" rectangles to make the borders of the Four Patch blocks. Unlike Summer Warmth, the Four Patch block borders are made from assorted prints. Make 18 blocks.

Four-Patch block.
Make 18.

ASSEMBLING THE QUILT TOP

1. Arrange the Sixteen Patch blocks and the Four Patch blocks into seven rows of five blocks each, following the layout diagram above right.

2. Sew the blocks into rows, pressing the seam allowances toward the Four Patch blocks. Sew the rows together to form the pieced center of the quilt.

3. Sew the green floral 4½"-wide strips end to end to make a continuous strip. Measure the quilt through the center from bottom to top and cut two strips to that measurement. Sew the strips to the sides of the quilt and press seam allowances toward the border strips.

4. Measure the quilt through the center from side to side, including the borders added in step 3. Cut two strips from the remainder of the long strip to that measurement. Sew the strips to the top and bottom of the quilt. Press the seam allowances toward the border strips.

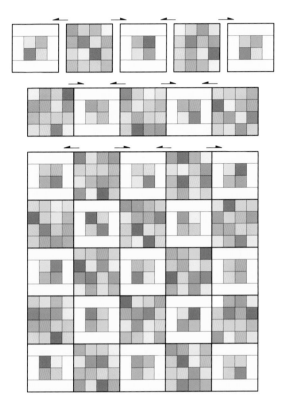

FINISHING THE QUILT

1. If necessary, mark your quilt for quilting. Layer the top with batting and backing; baste.

2. Hand or machine quilt as desired. Elissa machine quilted flowers and loops in a continuous design using her long-arm quilting machine.

3. Add a hanging sleeve if you intend to hang your quilt.

4. Using the diagonally striped strips and referring to "Straight-Grain Binding" on page 11 as needed, bind your quilt.

5. Label your quilt.

About the Authors

Heather Willms and Elissa Willms are a mother/daughter design team and co-owners of Hopscotch Quilt Shop in Coaldale, Alberta, Canada. Visit their shop on the Web at www.hopscotchquiltshop.com.

Elissa opened Hopscotch Quilt Shop when she was 15 years old. The shop was open on Saturdays and two afternoons a week for the first year of operation. Each year one more afternoon was added to the shop hours. After completing high school, Elissa spent the winter in England and traveling in Europe. On her return, she opened the shop full time. When not managing the shop and designing; Elissa likes to read, travel, and entertain Chloe, the family dog.

Heather teaches grade 5 at a local public school and helps Elissa with the shop. She is married to Lorne, and they have two children, Oliver and Elissa. When not teaching and quilting, Heather enjoys reading, hiking, and hanging out with Lorne.

Heather and Elissa's first book, *Christmas Quilts From Hopscotch* was published in the summer of 2008 by Martingale & Company.

Elissa and Heather

THERE'S MORE ONLINE!

Learn more about Elissa and Heather's shop at www.hopscotchquiltshop.com. Find more great books about quilting, knitting, crochet and more at www.martingale-pub.com.

Acknowledgments

Our thanks to:

For art lessons, music lessons, and unending encouragement in my creative endeavors—thanks Mom and Dad! ~ Heather

Karen Young, again, our quilts are safe in your hands! Thank you for doing an awesome job on both quilts in this book.

Dora Blue: thanks for stitching down those last three bindings! We love having you as a part of our lives!

Our staff, teachers, and customers; thank you for your encouragement and patience as we have worked on this book. Without you, there would be no Hopscotch Quilt Shop!

Moda United Notions for providing the fabric for "Circling the Patch" and the queen-size "Japanese Train Tiles." You're always quick and generous about sharing new and unavailable fabric with us.

Wonderfil Threads for supplying some of the thread used in our samples. Your customer service is second to none, and we love working with you.

Martingale & Company for believing in our ideas, even before they have reached their final evolution. We love the staff at Martingale and always look forward to when our paths will cross.

Robin Strobel for taking on the editing of our second book. You have been terrific to work with and have allowed us many opportunities for input and ideas.